BEFORE

THEY TURN

TWELVE

BEFORE

THEY TURN

TWELVE

Helping Children Gain a Testimony of the Lord's Standards

Deborah Pace Rowley

DESERET
BOOK

SALT LAKE CITY, UTAH

Library of Congress Cataloging-in-Publication Data

Rowley, Deborah Pace.
    Before they turn twelve : helping children gain a testimony of the Lord's standards / Deborah Pace Rowley.
      p.   cm.
    ISBN 978-1-59038-847-1
    1. Church of Jesus Christ of Latter-day Saints—Study and teaching.   2. Mormon Church—Study and teaching.
3. Christian education of children.
I. Title.
    BX8610.R69 2007
    248.8'450882893—dc22   2007037403

Printed in the United States of America
Malloy Lithographing Incorporated, Ann Arbor, MI

10   9   8   7   6   5   4   3   2   1

CONTENTS

INTRODUCTION

*Learn wisdom in thy youth; yea, learn in thy youth to keep
the commandments of God.—Alma 37:35*

Throughout the Church, when young people turn twelve years of age, they receive a small booklet entitled *For the Strength of Youth*. This booklet is given to them by their bishop or youth leaders and outlines the Lord's standards for behavior. In the booklet, the prophet and his counselors have given wonderful and timely direction in eighteen different areas. Each young person is encouraged to read and study the booklet and commit to live by its standards.

While the booklet is entitled *For the Strength of Youth,* its message is for everyone. No matter our age, we all have a duty to our Heavenly Father that includes standards he expects us to live by. We do not grow into the standards or grow too old for them. Wouldn't it be wonderful if all the adults in the Church would live worthy of these standards, just as they expect their teenagers to do? We should all "choose only entertainment and media that uplift [us]" (*For the Strength of Youth,* p. 17) We should all remember that "Sunday is not a holiday or a day for recreation or athletic events" (p. 33). We can all "live with a spirit of thanksgiving" (p. 6) and "seek to be . . . peacemakers" (p. 10).

The *For the Strength of Youth* booklet is not *just* for teenagers. The premise behind this book is that it should be introduced to our children *before* they turn twelve. A speaker once compared our children's lives to a basketball game. The children are the players; each parent is a coach. During the first eight minutes of the game, the opposing team is not even allowed on the court. Knowing these rules, wouldn't you have your players stand directly underneath the basket and shoot nonstop for those eight minutes? Potentially, you could be so far ahead after eight minutes that the opposing team could never catch up.

This is the situation our Heavenly Father has blessed us with in teaching our children. For eight years Satan is prevented from tempting or influencing them. If we teach them regularly, hold family home evening consistently, and read the scriptures faithfully during those critical early years, our children can be so strong and grounded in the gospel that Satan will have a hard time catching up.

It wouldn't be very wise coaching to let the players spend those first eight minutes lounging on the bench, talking to friends in the stands, or dribbling the ball around midcourt. Sure, at the eight-minute mark the score would be zero to zero. But it wouldn't take long to fall behind against such a determined opponent and losing the game would be a real possibility. This isn't a chance we can afford to take with our children. The stakes are so incredibly high and the opposition is so incredibly fierce.

How much stronger will a young man be when he has learned the Lord's standards at six or eight or ten? How much stronger will a young woman be who has grown up knowing the expectations her parents, her prophet, and her Heavenly Father have for her life? Introducing the *For the Strength of Youth* booklet to children when they are five or eight or eleven provides an incredible advantage. They will learn these standards when the peer pressure to break them is relatively nonexistent. They will gain a testimony of the standards and feel a desire to follow them when they are taught about this booklet during their formative years. This testimony and desire will follow them throughout their teenage years and into adulthood.

One stake president counseled, "If you want your children to marry well, teach them to live *For the Strength of Youth*." In a recent conversation with my sixteen-year-old niece, she expressed disappointment with a friend who, while in the backseat on a double date, began to kiss her boyfriend very heavily. Doesn't she know *For the Strength of Youth*? my niece wondered.

Don't they know *For the Strength of Youth*? That is a million-dollar question. Knowing, understanding, and living the principles taught in this booklet are the keys to remaining righteous and unspotted in an increasingly evil world. The *For the Strength of Youth* booklet is a gold mine, a hidden treasure, in just forty-two short pages.

The purpose of this book is to help you teach your children ages five to twelve about this wonderful booklet entitled *For the Strength of Youth*. There are stories and activities for each of the standards listed in the booklet. If you have teenage children these activities will also work for them, especially if they have younger brothers and sisters. One good idea is to put teenagers in charge of presenting these stories or object lessons to their younger siblings. They will learn much more when they are the teachers and will be blessed as they bear testimony of these standards to others.

Family home evening is the perfect time to teach about these standards. You could teach one topic in this book each Monday night for several months. Or you might choose to spend two family nights completing all the activities listed for each standard. *Before They Turn Twelve* can also be used on Sundays, during dinnertime discussions, as part of a family council, to prepare Primary talks, or in many other settings.

It is never too early or too late to learn about the standards outlined in *For the Strength of Youth*. As the First Presidency states in the opening message of the booklet, "We promise that as you keep these standards and live by the truths in the scriptures, you will be able to do your life's work with greater wisdom and skill and bear trials with greater courage. You will have the help of the Holy Ghost. You will feel good about yourself and will be a positive influence in the lives of others. You will be worthy to go to the temple to receive holy ordinances. These blessings and many more can be yours" (pp. 2–3). What more could we possibly want for our children?

It is my testimony that we can lay claim to these blessings by following the prophet and doing our part. I know Heavenly Father will bless us as we prayerfully plan ways to teach the inspired booklet *For the Strength of Youth* to our children.

Tips for Using This Book

Since all the lessons in the book are based on the *For the Strength of Youth* booklet, you will need one copy for each family member. The booklet is available at no cost through the Church Distribution Center or on-line at www.ldscatalog.com.

Read each lesson through on Sunday so you can see what you will need to prepare or purchase for Monday night.

Become familiar with the stories (including the stories from the scriptures) included in the lessons so you can retell them in your own words or read them fluently. Try to use some kind of visual aid for each story or have your children illustrate the story before the lesson.

Try out the refreshment suggestions. The treats are usually related to the lesson and can add another tasty teaching opportunity.

Don't miss any opportunity to bear your testimony. It might feel awkward at first, but sharing your testimony is the single most important thing you can do in teaching these principles.

Be patient with the kids who don't seem to be paying attention. They are getting more out of each lesson than you realize.

Most of all, have fun!

Lesson 1

MESSAGE FROM THE FIRST PRESIDENCY

Activity: Treasure Hunt

Before beginning this activity, you will need to hide a treat along with a picture of Heavenly Father and Jesus under a pillow on the parent's bed.

Explain to the family that they are going to search for a very valuable treasure, but they will each need a treasure map. Hand each family member a copy of the booklet *For the Strength of Youth*. Tell them this is the treasure map. Show them the Treasure Map Code. The sequence of numbers refers to the page number of the booklet, the line number, and then the word number on each page. For example, the first word, "seek," is found on the 10th page, the 17th line, and is the 6th word on that line. It is important to note that each section begins with a scripture and that the scripture lines are included in the line total. The title headings (such as "Family") are not. You may want to let your older children try to figure out the code on their own or with only a few hints from you.

Treasure Map Code

Word 1: 10–17–6
Word 2: 9–4–11
Word 3: 21–7–3
Word 4: 16–21–7
Word 5: 23–9–3
Word 6: 24–12–2
Word 7: 6–9–3

Once the clues have been decoded, the answer should read: "Seek it where parents say their prayers."

As a family, retrieve the treasure and share the treat. Take a moment to bear your testimony that the greatest treasure we receive is eternal life and the ability to return to live with Heavenly Father and Jesus Christ again. The *For the Strength of Youth* booklet led them to treats, but it will also lead them to the greatest treasure—eternal life with Heavenly Father. The booklet is the treasure map that Jesus has provided for us through his prophet.

For the Strength of Youth

Have each family member write his or her name on the outside of the *For the Strength of Youth* booklet. Invite them to look closely at the cover. Then discuss the following questions: What do the title and subtitle mean to you? What does the picture on the front tell you about this booklet? Open to the first page. Why is there a picture of Jesus on the first page? Before you turn to the table of contents, ask the family to guess some of the topics that might be included. Turn to the contents page and read the list of topics together. Were any of the topics guessed correctly?

Turn to the next page and read what the First Presidency has said in the beginning of the *For the Strength of Youth* booklet. Read the first paragraph out loud and substitute the names of each of your children in place of the phrase "young men and women" in the first sentence. For example: "Our beloved Sarah, Michael, and Lisa, we have great confidence in you. You are choice spirits who have come forth in this day when the responsibilities and opportunities, as well as the temptations, are the greatest" (p. 2).

As a family identify and underline all the blessings that are promised when we follow the standards in this booklet. There are at least six mentioned. They are found in the third paragraph. The First Presidency also tells us that many more blessings are available to us when we keep these standards. List additional blessings as a family.

Story: Samuel the Lamanite

Before telling the story of Samuel the Lamanite, have a bag of large marshmallows on hand. The story of Samuel the Lamanite is found in Helaman, chapters 13 through 15. The following scriptures are significant: Helaman 13:2–6; 14:2–5, 9–11, 20–21, 29–31; 16:1–2. How we respond to the prophet's counsel is a good indication of how committed we are to the Lord.

Have Dad (or Mom or another family member) play the role of the prophet Samuel. He can stand on a table, at the top of the stairs, or somewhere else where he is higher than the rest of the family. He will then call out to the family, admonishing them to live gospel standards. The family, on the other hand, will role-play the part of the wicked Nephites who refused to hearken to the prophet. They will refuse to keep the standards and will attempt to hit the prophet (Dad) with stones (marshmallows).

For example, Dad could say, "The Lord commands you to dress modestly." The family would respond, "No! We don't care what the Lord wants. We won't dress modestly!" Dad could say, "Don't date until you're sixteen." The family could shout back, "We will date when we are fifteen if we want to!"

At the end of the activity, ask the family how it felt to reject the prophet. Read in the Book of Mormon about the consequences the Nephites faced for rejecting Samuel the Lamanite and stoning other prophets in their day (3 Nephi 9:1–4, 10–12).

The consequences for not following the prophet today are just as serious. The Savior is coming soon and we need to be prepared. The prophet is like a watchman on a tower. Just like Samuel the Lamanite, he is standing on higher ground and can see farther ahead. He is a prophet, seer, and revelator, which means that Heavenly Father shows him the future and lets him know what we need to do to be prepared. Even if we aren't physically throwing rocks at the prophet, we are still rejecting him when we do not do what he says.

Game: Knock Your Socks Off

Satan tries very hard to get us to break the standards found in *For the Strength of Youth*. If he can convince us to ignore, forget about, or break these standards even in little ways, he will have succeeded. We need to strive every day to defend and protect ourselves by living these standards. To illustrate this point, play the game "Knock Your Socks Off."

Have family members remove their shoes and get on their hands and knees on the living room floor. At the count of three, family members crawl around a designated area, trying to pull other people's socks off at the same time that they try to defend their own feet and keep their own socks on. Once both of your socks have been removed, you are eliminated and must watch the proceedings from the couch. The winner is the person who is still left with at least one sock on at the end of the game. Just like this game, the goal of life is to keep our socks—or in other words, our standards—on at all times.

Commitment

At the end of each lesson, bear your testimony of the standards you have talked about. Just as the First Presidency knows that these standards are true, you also know that the standards are true. Express your personal commitment to the prophet and your desire to follow him.

If you feel inspired to do so, you may want your children to express their commitment to live these standards. Younger children could put a sticker or draw a smiley face on page 2 or 3 of the *For the Strength of Youth* booklet. Older family members could choose to write their feelings about the prophet and their commitment to follow him on these pages or in their journals.

Treat: Rice Krispie Treats

Follow the recipe on the cereal box and use a bag of marshmallows to make Rice Krispie Treats. Add M&Ms or spread peanut butter or melted chocolate chips across the top for a fun variation. Remind the family that marshmallows were also used to throw at the prophet. Which was a better use of the marshmallows? This example can remind us that following the prophet is much more rewarding than complaining about his counsel or murmuring about the Lord's standards.

Lesson 2

AGENCY AND ACCOUNTABILITY

Object Lesson: Choice and Consequence

Prepare ahead by writing the word "Choice" on one piece of paper and the word "Consequence" on another. Attach the two pieces of paper with a thin white piece of thread or clear fishing line at least two feet long. Lay the two pieces of paper on the ground beforehand so that the string is not visible.

Ask a family member to pick up the word "Choice" and hold it in the air. When they do this the word "Consequence" will follow. Say, "But I didn't want you to pick up 'Consequence'; I just wanted you to pick up 'Choice.'" Let someone else try. Make a big deal about just picking up the one word. Then explain that you can't make a choice without having a consequence—the two always go together. When you are accountable, you realize that your choices caused the consequence and you accept responsibility. You do not blame other people for your choices or the consequences.

Activity: Multiple Choices

Designate three corners of the room as A, B, and C by hanging up small signs. Read a choice to the family and then read three consequences. If family members think that A is the correct consequence for that choice, they should run to the A corner. If they think B is the logical consequence, they should run to the B corner, and so on.

Choice 1: You break the living room lamp and tell your Mom the truth when she asks who did it.

Consequences:

    A: You will have to earn money to fix the lamp, but Mom will be proud of you for being honest. You will feel good inside.

    B: You will have to keep lying to cover up the real story.

    C: You will have to move and live with a different family.

Choice 2: You disobey Mom and eat lots of yummy cookies before dinner.

Consequences:

    A: Mom will feel happy and will make more cookies for you.

    B: You will feel good inside and your body will be healthy.

    C: You will feel bad inside and dinner won't taste good, plus Mom will be upset.

Choice 3: You stay at your friend's house to watch a bad movie even though you know you should leave.

Consequences:

    A: The Holy Ghost will stay with you.

    B: You will be able to forget about the bad parts as soon as the movie is over.

    C: The bad parts will keep coming back to your mind, and you will have a yucky feeling inside. The Holy Ghost will have to leave.

Choice 4: You pay your tithing even though you really want a new toy and will have to wait to buy it.

Consequences:

    A: Heavenly Father will be pleased by your obedience and will bless you. You will feel good inside.

    B: An angel will leave the toy under your pillow.

    C: Your parents will be mad because they wanted to play with that toy too.

Choice 5: You obey Dad and stay out of the street when you are playing outside.

Consequences:

    A: You will be locked in your room and will never be able to play outside again.

    B: You will feel good inside and Dad will be able to trust you to play outside.

    C: You will get hit by a car.

Choice 6: You drink a can of beer when a friend dares you to try some.

Consequences:

    A: You will be worthy to go to the temple to perform baptisms for the dead.

    B: You will be given more courage to stand up to your friend next time.

    C: You might feel sick, you could become addicted, and you will feel ashamed inside.

Story: Amber Accountable and Brad Blame

Plan ahead by copying and coloring the pictures of Amber Accountable and Brad Blame (see pages 15–16). Write the story phrases on individual word strips. Then lay down the word strips so that they are visible to the family.

Story Phrases

She did it.	It was me.
I am sorry.	I should have listened better.
I made a mistake.	I couldn't help it.
I won't do that again.	It was my fault.
You said I could.	I should have known better.
I didn't know.	You didn't tell me to.
I didn't do it.	I did it.
It wasn't my fault.	

Tell the story of Amber Accountable and Brad Blame. When the story asks what Brad and Amber say to their mother, ask the family to choose a word strip that would fit and lay that word strip on the picture of Amber or the picture of Brad. There is not one specific word strip that fits each situation. The only rule is that Amber will be accountable and Brad will blame others.

Amber Accountable and Brad Blame

Amber and Brad were twins. They looked alike and they liked the same things. They were best friends and were always together. But there was one difference between Amber and her brother. Amber was accountable for her actions, while Brad blamed everyone else.

One morning when Amber and Brad woke up, Mom was rushing around in her bathrobe. "Hurry, Amber! Hurry, Brad!" Mom called as she whizzed by. "You need to eat your breakfast and help clean up the house right away because my visiting teachers will be here soon." Mom went to get dressed while Brad and Amber got out some cereal. The twins liked it when Mom's visiting teachers came over because sometimes they brought a treat for the whole family to share.

When Mom rushed out of her room fifteen minutes later, Amber and Brad were watching cartoons. Mom looked at the kitchen. The milk and bowls and cereal were still all over the counter. "Kids," Mom said, "why didn't you take care of your mess?"

What did Brad say? What did Amber say?

After Amber and Brad cleaned up the kitchen, Mom asked them to get dressed and make their beds. Amber got dressed and started to make her bed until she found a book under the covers and started to read. Brad found his action figures instead of his clothes in his dresser and started to play. Mom walked in a few minutes later. She looked a little mad, but she said calmly, "Brad, Amber, are you doing what I asked you to do?"

What did Amber say? What did Brad say?

Amber and Brad quickly made their beds with Mom's help and then began to play quietly together. Brad liked to pretend that he was a superhero, rescuing Amber's dolls. But when he was pretending to fly with one of the dolls, the doll's arm fell off.

What did Brad say?

Amber got so mad that she hit her brother and then they both started to yell and cry. Mom came running to see what the matter was and asked Brad and Amber what had happened.

What did Amber say? What did Brad say?

Mom said that Dad could fix the doll when he got home. Then the doorbell rang and Mom had to go answer it. It was her visiting teachers. Mom poked her head back in the bedroom to ask the kids to please play quietly and to not bother her until her visiting teachers had left. The visit seemed to take a long time, and Amber really wanted a snack. She got hungrier and hungrier. Finally she went out to the living room and tugged on Mom's sleeve. Mom said, "Amber, I am almost done visiting with these sisters. You know you weren't supposed to bother me until they were gone."

What did Amber say?

Mother smiled and said that she would get Amber a snack as soon as her visiting teachers left. Amber went back to the bedroom, and Brad was jumping on his bed. Amber started jumping on her bed, too. Then they started throwing a soccer ball between them. The ball bounced off the wall and hit the lamp on the nightstand. The lamp fell to the floor with a crash. Mom came rushing in.

What did Amber say? What did Brad say?

Mom was sad that the twins broke the lamp, but she was more upset with Brad for not accepting responsibility for his actions. "Brad, when you won't admit that you have done something wrong, you can't repent and make it right. You are the one who is responsible for your actions. No one else is to blame. You need to learn to be accountable." Mom helped Brad clean up the broken lamp while Amber straightened the beds. Then Mom shared the cookies her visiting teachers had brought. When they were finished, Brad and Amber went outside to play. . . .

What do you think will happen next? Make up your own story about the twins and use the rest of the phrases that Amber Accountable and Brad Blame say.

For the Strength of Youth

Read the counsel of the prophet under the topic "Agency and Accountability." Discuss why it is important to be accountable for our choices. Then read 2 Nephi 2:27 and Matthew 25:14–29. How does the parable of the talents relate to agency and accountability? How does it apply to us?

Commitment

Bear your testimony that exercising our agency wisely and being accountable is one of the most important things that we can do on earth. Heavenly Father sent us to earth to see how we will use our agency. We will never be very good at using our agency if we are always blaming others for our choices. One day we will stand before God to give an accounting of our choices on earth. This will be a wonderful experience if we have learned to be accountable.

Invite younger children to place a sticker or draw a smiley face on page 4 of the *For the Strength of Youth* booklet. Older family members could choose to write their feelings about agency and their commitment to be accountable on the bottom of that page or in their journals.

Treat: Chocolate Fondue

Serve chocolate fondue with lots of "choices" that can be dipped into the melted chocolate. Some fun fondue dippers include doughnuts or angel food cake cut into pieces, graham cracker sticks, vanilla wafers, pretzels, marshmallows, strawberries, bananas, pineapple, mandarin oranges, and maraschino cherries. Come up with more dipping ideas of your own.

AMBER ACCOUNTABLE

BRAD BLAME

Lesson 3

GRATITUDE

Story: The Ten Lepers

Lepers were cast out of society because they suffered from a terrible disease. They couldn't live with their families. They even had to ring a bell to let people know they were coming so that everyone could get out of the way.

Tell the children to imagine that they are lepers. (Let one child know ahead of time that he or she can be the grateful leper.) Tell the story of the ten lepers found in Luke 17:12–19. Hold up a picture of the Savior and ask the children to imagine that when Jesus came to their village and saw the lepers, he didn't run away like everyone else. He healed them.

Ask the child designated as the grateful leper how he or she would feel to be healed by Jesus. Did it feel good to say "Thank you"? How did the other children who didn't thank Jesus feel inside when they heard another leper express gratitude? As a family, discuss the importance of gratitude and share some examples of times when you did or did not express gratitude.

Object Lesson: A Pebble in the Shoe

Give each family member a small pebble to put in one of their shoes and a piece of candy to eat. Have them walk around the living room, eating the candy and feeling the pebble. Ask them which experience they noticed more. Would the candy have been more enjoyable to eat without the pebble as a distraction? Explain that when we are ungrateful and complain, it is like we have a pebble in our shoe. We don't fully experience the sweet blessings that Heavenly Father has given us, and we don't notice them as easily.

For the Strength of Youth

Read what the prophet says about gratitude in the booklet. Read Doctrine and Covenants 78:19 and Doctrine and Covenants 46:32, and discuss why God has commanded us to be grateful.

Game: Alphabet Gratitude

Write the twenty-six letters of the alphabet onto a sheet of paper and cut them out. Place all the letters in a bowl, and have a family member draw out a letter. Give the family members one minute to write down—individually or in teams—all the things they are grateful for that begin with that letter. Award one point for each item listed. Choose another letter and play again. Draw as many letters out of the bowl as you want. To increase the challenge, award a point only for the blessings that no one else in the family has written down.

Activity: The Thanking Chair

Designate one chair at the dinner table as the Thanking Chair. Whoever is sitting in that chair tells five things that he or she is grateful for. Take turns sitting in the Thanking Chair. For added fun, use a silly hat as the Thanking Cap, and place it on the person who shares his or her five grateful things for the night. You may also want to use the Thanking Cap throughout the week to encourage spontaneous moments of gratitude.

Commitment

Bear your testimony of the power of gratitude in helping us to be happy and show our love to Heavenly Father. You may want to have younger children put a sticker or draw a smiley face on the gratitude page in the *For the Strength of Youth* booklet. Older family members could choose to write their feelings about gratitude and their commitment to be more grateful on page 6 of the booklet or in their journals.

Treat: "Count Your Blessings" Candy

Serve a variety of small candies and call them "Count Your Blessings" candy. Family members must name a blessing for each piece of candy they eat.

Lesson 4

EDUCATION

Activity: Puppet Show

Copy the picture of the bee (see pages 23–24), and provide your family with brown paper sacks and crayons for making hand puppets. Color and cut out the bees and tape them to the sack to make hand puppets. Assign parts and use the puppets as you tell the story about Buzby the Bee. After finishing the story, ask the family the following questions: Was Buzby glad that he went to school? Why? Why is learning important?

Buzby the Bee

Puppet Show Parts:
Buzby, the little bee who doesn't want to go to school
Buzby's mother
Buzby's teacher
The other bees in the class

Buzby didn't want to go to Happy Hive Bee School. He was happy staying home and buzzing around all day with his mom. "I won't go!" Buzby said as the first day of school drew closer and closer.

"You need to give Bee School a try," encouraged Buzby's mom. "You just might like the taste of it."

Buzby knew that he wouldn't like the taste, smell, or sight of Bee School. But on the day school started, Buzby flew high above the classroom—just to take a look. Before Buzby realized what had happened, he had flown close enough to hear the teacher say, "Class, you have learned how to gather nectar from flowers; now it is your turn to experiment."

The students flew to the surrounding flowers and began to sip the delicious nectar. "Yum, yum, yum," Buzby heard the little bees say. "This is delicious."

"Wait for me," yelled Buzby. "I don't know how to get nectar out of flowers. Can someone teach me?" The bee school teacher quickly flew over and taught Buzby about nectar so that he could taste some too.

For the rest of the year, Buzby buzzed over to school every morning with a smile on his face. He learned about nectar; he learned how to use his stinger; and he learned how to fill the honeycombs in a beehive. That was his favorite part. Did you know that what bees do best is make honey? And Buzby just so happened to be the best Happy Hive honey maker of them all.

So the next time you have some sweet, syrupy honey that dribbles off your chin, think of Buzby. It could be that he made it, and if he did, remember that he learned how to make it that sweet at school.

Oh, and the next time you see a bee in your classroom, let him fly peacefully out the window. It might be Buzby, flying by to learn something new.

P.S. I bet you didn't know that it is a Jewish tradition for parents to put a little bit of honey on their baby's first book. That way the baby will taste the sweetness of the book and love learning and reading for his or her whole life.

For the Strength of Youth

Read in the *For the Strength of Youth* booklet why the Lord wants us to learn and to gain an education. Emphasize that we can find joy in learning at church, at school, and at home. When we don't want to learn or when we refuse to learn, we are like Buzby and we cannot accomplish our mission here on earth. Read Alma 37:35 and Doctrine and Covenants 88:77–80.

Discussion

Ask the family three questions:

Question 1: How do you make a blade of grass?

Question 2: How many stars are in the sky?

Question 3: Have any birds fallen out of trees and died anywhere on earth today?

We can't answer any of these questions.

Who does know the answer to these questions?

Jesus Christ does. He created the earth and everything on it. He knows how many stars are in the sky. He knows about the fall of the sparrow, and he knows about each of us. Jesus knows everything. But did you know that we have been commanded to become like Jesus? He has promised us that we can be like him and know what he knows. Does this mean that we need to keep learning? Yes! Do even Moms and Dads need to keep learning? Yes! We all need to learn from the scriptures, from good books, from going to school and to church, and from studying, listening, observing, and working hard. The Holy Ghost will help us get the knowledge that we need, "line upon line, precept upon precept" (2 Nephi 28:30). We will keep learning even after we die.

Activity: The Six Bs Relay

Remind the family that the prophet thinks that learning is very important. "Be smart" was one of President Gordon B. Hinckley's Six Bs, and he even established the Perpetual Education Fund to help young men and young women get the education they need.

For the Six Bs Relay, family members will run to a certain part of the house, say one of the six phrases, perform a simple action that will help them remember that "B," then run to the next part of the house. Make it a timed obstacle course to see who can finish the relay fastest, or make it a relay with two teams racing against each other. Start at the front door.

B #1: Run to the dining room and touch your lips while mouthing the words "Thank you." Shout out, "Be grateful."

B #2: Run to a bedroom and kneel down and fold your arms. Whisper, "Be prayerful."

B #3: Run to the kitchen and bow your head. Say, "Be humble."

B #4: Run to the home office or stand beside a bookshelf. Point to your brain and declare, "Be smart."

B #5: Run to the bathroom and rub your hands together as if you were washing them. Say, "Be clean."

B #6: Run to the living room, place your hand over your heart, and promise to "Be true."

Run back to the front door. The first person or team to touch the door wins the relay.

Commitment

Bear your testimony of the importance of education. Share why education is important to you and explain the blessings your education has brought into your life. Congratulate each family member for the things that he or she has learned during the past year. Let each person know that he or she is smart and capable of learning all the things that Heavenly Father wants his children to know. Encourage the family to keep learning every day.

You may want to invite younger family members to place a sticker or draw a smiley face on page 9 of the *For the Strength of Youth* booklet. Older family members could choose to write their feelings about learning and their future goals about gaining an education in the booklet or in their journals.

Treat: Scones with Honey

Make scones by thawing Rhodes Frozen Rolls. Have each family member participate in rolling or stretching out each roll until it is about the size of a hand. Fry the rolls in hot oil, turning once, until golden brown. Eat the warm scones with honey. As you eat the honey, discuss Buzby the Bee's lesson: hard work and learning will bring about delicious results.

head

wings

BUZBY THE BEE

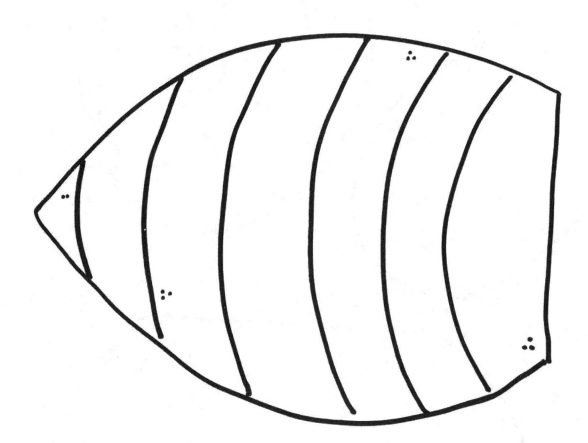

body

Lesson 5

FAMILY

Object Lesson: Name Tags

Before family home evening begins, make two name tags—one negative and one positive—for each family member. On the negative name tags use the following words or other negative labels of your choice: *Bully, Name Caller, Hitter, Whiner, Tease, Fighter.* On the positive name tags, write the following words or other positive labels of your choice: *Gives Compliments, Kind Friend, Good Sharer, Obedient Helper, Loving Hugger, Peacemaker.*

Have the family imagine that Jesus is coming for a visit. Tell them that you have made a special name tag for each person. Have the family members close their eyes. Tape a negative name tag on each family member. Ask them to open their eyes and read the name tag. Ask them how they feel wearing a name tag that says "Fighter" or "Name Caller" or "Tease."

Then ask each family member what labels they would like to be wearing when Jesus comes. Hand out the positive name tags to each person. Ask if they like these names better. Would they be ashamed or proud to have Jesus come over while they were wearing these name tags? But are these name tags true? How often do we do live up to qualities described on the positive name tags?

For the Strength of Youth

While reading what the prophet says about families in the *For the Strength of Youth* booklet, have the family members stand every time they hear the word "be." Stop and make note of these phrases: "Be cheerful, helpful, and considerate of others"; "Seek to be a peacemaker rather than to tease, fight, and quarrel"; and "Be willing to help in the home with chores that need to be done." Discuss how your family is doing in following the prophet's counsel. Read Ephesians 6:1–3.

Story: Who Is in Our House Today? A Hide-and-Seek Story

Copy and color the contention monsters and the angels (see page 30). Cut them out and hide them before telling the story. Hide the contention monsters in a child's room, the living room, and the bathroom. Hide the angels in the kitchen, the parents' bedroom, and the laundry room.

Define the word *contention* if it is a word that your children don't know. Then tell the story "Who Is in Our House Today?"

Who Is in Our House Today? A Hide-and-Seek Story

My name is Luke, and my sister's name is Sarah. We are just one year and twenty-two days apart, so sometimes people think we are twins. But I am older and taller, and Sarah has more freckles and is missing one of her front teeth.

Sarah is okay for a little sister. Most of the time we get along. We hardly fight at all, actually. That is because we had one really unusual day. On this particular day, Sarah and I thought that Mom had flipped. It all started out like this:

I was playing with my new building system in my room, and Sarah was playing dolls in her room. Things were pretty peaceful. Then I maneuvered my cool new machine into Sarah's room and it started to pick up Sarah's doll's clothes with these cool pinchers that I had built onto the front. That made Sarah mad, and she kicked over the machine. That made *me* mad and we started to fight.

Suddenly Mom called from the kitchen, "Who let the contention monster into this house? Didn't I tell you he wasn't invited?" We looked at each other. The contention monster? What was Mom talking about? There wasn't a monster in the house. Sarah lifted up the ruffle on her comforter and looked under the bed just in case. No monster there. We didn't believe in them, anyway.

Pause to let the children find the contention monster hidden in the child's bedroom.

I didn't think too much more about this monster thing until it was three o'clock and time for my favorite show. I ran into the living room and dove for the beanbag chair—the most comfortable spot in the house. The only problem was that Sarah was already there. This resulted in a little fight over the chair. Our voices got louder and then someone pushed someone else, and Mom entered the room.

"I knew I heard that contention monster!" She grabbed the beanbag chair and looked underneath it. "I wish I could find that horrible beast," murmured Mom as she walked out of the room. Sarah's eyes got really big and she stared at me, but I just shrugged. Sarah looked under the couch before the show started, but there was nothing there.

Pause to let the children find the contention monster hidden in the living room.

After the show, we went outside. There was this great mud pile in the corner of the garden where Dad hadn't planted anything, and we built a mud castle for worms and ladybugs. When we came to the back door, Mom took one look at us and sent us straight to the bathroom to wash up. The only problem was that there was only one sink in the bathroom and two kids. My elbow kind of blocked Sarah and she got mad and said that she needed to go first because she was a girl. Before we knew it, we were in another fight, and Mom appeared.

"All right," she said, holding a big spoon above her head. "Come out this minute, Contention Monster, or I will come in after you. I mean it. You are not welcome in his home anymore." Then Mom banged her spoon on the side of the shower door and rattled some cupboards before she left.

Pause to let the children find the contention monster hidden in the bathroom.

We were speechless. What was up with Mom? She had told us there were no such things as monsters when we were little, and now she was saying that a contention monster was in our house? Was she crazy? We thought maybe we should tell Dad about it. In the meantime, I figured we had better take care of Mom and not do anything to upset her anymore. I told Sarah my idea and she agreed. So while Mom was on the phone in her bedroom, Sarah set the table and I wiped up the mud that we had tracked over the floor.

Mom was so surprised when she came out of her room and found the clean floor and the table set for dinner that she almost fainted. She staggered back against the kitchen counter and said, "I can't believe it. Are there some angels in my kitchen now?" I just looked at Sarah and smiled.

Pause to let the children find the angel hidden in the kitchen.

Sarah followed me into the laundry room so I could put the dirty towels away that I had used to clean the floor. A clean basket of clothes was piled high in the center of the room. I looked at Sarah and she nodded. She was thinking the same thing. We both sat down and started to fold the clothes that Mom had washed earlier that day.

We heard Mom calling from the kitchen, "Are there angels in my laundry room? I can hear you in there. I don't know who let you in but you are welcome to stay!" Sarah had to put her hand over her mouth to keep from giggling out loud. Monsters and angels—Mom was really going nuts.

Pause to let the children find the angel hidden in the laundry room.

Dad came home right after that and he was impressed when Mom told him about the angels who had helped in the kitchen and in the laundry room. I decided we should wait to talk to Dad about Mom's behavior until we could get him alone. After dinner, Dad helped Mom clean up, and then he went into his room to watch a basketball game. We followed him into his room, and Sarah climbed onto his lap to give him a hug. Mom came in and asked, "Did you hear some angels in here, honey?"

Dad shook his head.

"That's strange. I was sure I heard some love coming from this room," Mom said.

"You did," Sarah said excitedly, as she jumped up and hugged Mom. "It was coming from me."

"Thank you for the hug, sweetie," Mom responded. "I love you too. But where could those angels be?" She lifted up her pillow and looked underneath, then started searching her closet. That is when Sarah and I slipped out and went to bed without being asked. We never did talk to Dad because Mom started acting normal the next day.

Sarah and I still try to help and not fight and stuff just in case Mom starts seeing monsters and angels again.

Let the children hunt for the last angel hidden in the parents' bedroom.

When the story is finished and you have found all the hidden creatures, tell the family that when we fight it is like we are inviting a contention monster into our home. The monster might not be real, but the bad feelings are. And when bad feelings are present, the Holy Ghost has to leave and the spirit of the devil is present instead. When we are peacemakers it is like we are inviting angels into our home because the Holy Ghost can be with us, and the Spirit of Christ will be in our home.

Activity: Contention Monster Ball

Gather a beach ball, rubber ball, or plastic ball; newspaper; and tape for this activity.

Tell the family that instead of fighting against each other, you want to fight against the contention monster. Label the ball as the contention monster. You may even want to tape monster facial features or a funny wig to the ball to add to the fun.

Instruct everyone in the family to make their own "monster bopper" by rolling up 15 to 20 sheets of newspaper into a long tube. Wrap tape around the newspaper roll in several places to help it stay together. Divide the family into two teams and label two opposite areas of the play area or yard as goals. Each player uses his or her bopper to try to keep the ball out of their own goal and hit it into the opposing team's goal. Encourage teamwork, pointing out that defeating the contention monster is easier when you work together.

Commitment

Bear testimony of the importance of the family in Heavenly Father's plan. Share your faith that the Savior will come again and that you need to be prepared as a family to greet him. Let each person know that he or she is important to your family and that each one can be a peacemaker.

You may want younger children to draw a smiley face or put a sticker on page 10 in the *For the Strength of Youth* booklet. Older family members could choose to write their feelings about their family and their ideas on how to strengthen the family in the booklet or in their journals.

Treat: Famous Family Snack Mix

Create a special family snack mix by inviting each member of the family to choose a snack item to add to the bowl. Some ideas include pretzels, raisins, dry cereal, crackers, cranberries, nuts, mini-marshmallows, or M&Ms. When each person has added his or her snack, dive into the bowl together. Talk about how much better this snack mix is because everyone in the family contributed something. Families are the same way—they wouldn't be complete with even one family member missing. Write down the ingredients of your concoction so that you can make your famous family snack mix anytime you want.

CONTENTION MONSTERS

ANGELS

Lesson 6

FRIENDS

Story: The Magical Change in Pricklyville

Tell the story of "The Magical Change in Pricklyville." Whenever you say the words "cold prickly," family members have to poke the person next to them. Whenever you say the words "warm fuzzy," they have to hug the person next to them.

The Magical Change in Pricklyville

Once upon a time there was a village where everyone was grumpy and everyone was mean. Travelers went miles and miles out of their way to avoid it. The villagers fought with each other, called each other names, and gave each other cold pricklies all the time.

It was true, the children in this village were given two bags on the day they were born, one bag of cold pricklies and one bag of warm fuzzies. But in Pricklyville the only bag that got used was the cold one. And as you can imagine, cold pricklies made people feel cold and ugly and small. They hurt, and they made both the giver and the receiver feel bad, but they got handed out just the same. And if someone gave you a cold prickly, you just had to give one back. Unfortunately, there were always enough cold pricklies to go around.

At least there were until the day a stranger arrived in Pricklyville. As soon as he got into town, the village children gathered around him. They were too young to remember to avoid strangers, and they didn't know that strangers' cold pricklies were extremely cold. But this stranger didn't use his cold prickly bag. Maybe he didn't even have one, for no one ever saw it on his belt. Instead, he opened his warm fuzzy bag and handed out a warm fuzzy to each child. Many of the children had never received a warm fuzzy before. They were surprised at how warm and good it made them feel inside. So good, in fact, that they started to smile and laugh.

This made the grown-ups come running. What could that sound be? They saw the happy children and the happy stranger, but before any of the parents could get mad, the stranger handed out warm fuzzies to them too. Pretty soon the parents were smiling and saying nice things to each other.

Then the mayor arrived. He marched right up to the stranger and said in a not-so-nice voice, "Why are you handing out your warm fuzzies in our town?" The mayor reached in his vest pocket and pulled out the biggest, coldest cold prickly he had.

The stranger smiled at the mayor, took his cold prickly, and dropped it on the ground. Then he reached into his bag and gave the mayor back the biggest, warmest warm fuzzy anyone had ever seen.

"But, but, but," the mayor stuttered. "If you give your warm fuzzies to us, there won't be any left for you."

"Oh, didn't you know?" said the stranger in disbelief. "The bags are magic. The more warm fuzzies you give away, the more warm fuzzies you find in their place." With that, the stranger stood up, smiled, waved good-bye, and left town. But not before he had given away many more warm fuzzies and changed the town.

Travelers say that you can't get within a mile of the village now without being swamped with a flood of warm fuzzies. They even had to change the name to Fuzzyville. And the bags were indeed magic, for no one has run out of warm fuzzies yet, and the villagers love to laugh and hug and smile.

At the conclusion of the story, ask family members which type of person they would like to be around—the one who used his cold prickly bag or the one who used his warm fuzzy bag. Explain that even though we don't have actual bags of warm fuzzies or cold pricklies, it is like we are giving away these things when we make others feel happy or sad by our words and actions.

Activity: Choosing Friends Puzzle

Copy the pictures of the warm fuzzy and the cold prickly (see pages 36–37) onto the same color paper. Cut each picture into eight puzzle pieces. Write one of the following words or phrases on the back of each puzzle piece. On the cold prickly pieces write: *tells bad jokes, always in trouble, immodest, lies, swears, teases and puts down others, disobedient, dares you to do things you shouldn't do.* On the warm fuzzy pieces write: *clean conversation, good language, modest clothing, hardworking student, friendly and happy, makes good choices, kind to everyone, obedient to parents.* Mix up the two puzzles in one bag.

Tell the family that there are two puzzles inside the bag. The pieces are all mixed up, but you can separate them by reading the words on the back. If the back describes a quality of a good friend, put it in one pile. If the back describes a quality that wouldn't make someone a good friend, put it in the other. Once the puzzle pieces are separated, turn the pieces over and complete the pictures. Explain that this puzzle activity is a lot like choosing friends. We can't always tell just by looking at someone if they are going to be a good friend or not. We can't tell by the clothes they wear or by how cute or popular they are. We can't look to see if they are carrying a cold prickly bag or a warm fuzzy bag. What is important is how they treat others and how obedient they are to Heavenly Father's commandments. We can look at someone's actions to determine whether he or she will make a good friend.

For the Strength of Youth

Read what the prophet has said about friends in the *For the Strength of Youth* booklet. Notice all the words in the section that are warm fuzzy words (actions that create good feelings in others). Here are a few examples: "strengthen and encourage each other," "show interest," "care," "treat everyone with kindness and respect," "invite," "help them feel welcome and wanted," "strengthen them."

Read Matthew 25:40 and Alma 17:1–2.

Story: President Gordon B. Hinckley and Following the Crowd

Friends can be kind or mean, and they can influence us in good or bad ways. Here is a story about something that happened to President Gordon B. Hinckley when he was a boy. You can read this experience as it was written in President Hinckley's biography or tell it in your own words.

As [Gordon] prepared to enter the seventh grade, he and his friends looked forward to being the first class to occupy the new Roosevelt Junior High School. But when they reported to school, they learned that the building was already overcrowded and their class was being moved back to the elementary school for one more year. Gordon and his friends had already spent six years at Hamilton, and they felt they deserved something better than a sentence to another year with the lower grades. The following day they went "on strike" and played "hooky." When they returned to school the next day, the principal . . . greeted them at the front door and announced that they would be readmitted only after they supplied a letter of explanation from their parents. Ada [Gordon's mother] was not pleased when she learned what had transpired, and her note to the principal contained a rebuke that stung her eldest son. "Dear Mr. Stearns, Please excuse Gordon's absence yesterday. His action was simply an impulse to follow the crowd." He later explained, . . . "To have Mother classify me as one to do something just to follow the crowd cut me, and I made up my mind then and there that I would never do anything just to follow the crowd." (Sheri Dew, *Go Forward with Faith* [Salt Lake City: Deseret Book, 1996], 32)

Discussion

After hearing the story, discuss the following questions: Can our friends be good or bad for us? What would have happened to President Hinckley if he had kept following the crowd? How do you think the decision to make his own good choices and not just follow others influenced this future prophet?

We need to choose friends carefully and we also need to be a good friend to others. Remember that your brothers and sisters are your eternal friends. Do you give them warm fuzzies or cold pricklies?

Activity: Friendship Circle

Make a friendship circle. Have the family stand in a circle. Instruct each person to reach out with his or her left hand and take the hand of someone across the circle. Then grab the hand of someone else with your right hand. When you all have hold of two hands, the fun begins. The goal is to sort out the circle without ever letting go of each others' hands. You can climb over or go under people's arms, but you can't release your hands. The bond between good friends can be as unbreakable as this circle.

Commitment

Bear your testimony about the importance friends have had in your life and encourage family members to choose good friends. Express your faith that Heavenly Father will help your children choose true friends who will help them follow the Lord's standards. You may want to have younger members of the family draw a smiley face or put a sticker on page 13 in the *For the Strength of Youth* booklet. Older family members could choose to write their thoughts about friends and their commitment to choose good friends in the booklet or in their journals.

Treat: Warm Fuzzies

Hostess Snowballs make cute warm fuzzy treats, especially if you add candy eyes with a dab of frosting. For fun, you could set out a plate of cold prickly treats too—dill pickles with toothpicks poking out all over them, for example. Let the family choose which treat they would like!

WARM FUZZY

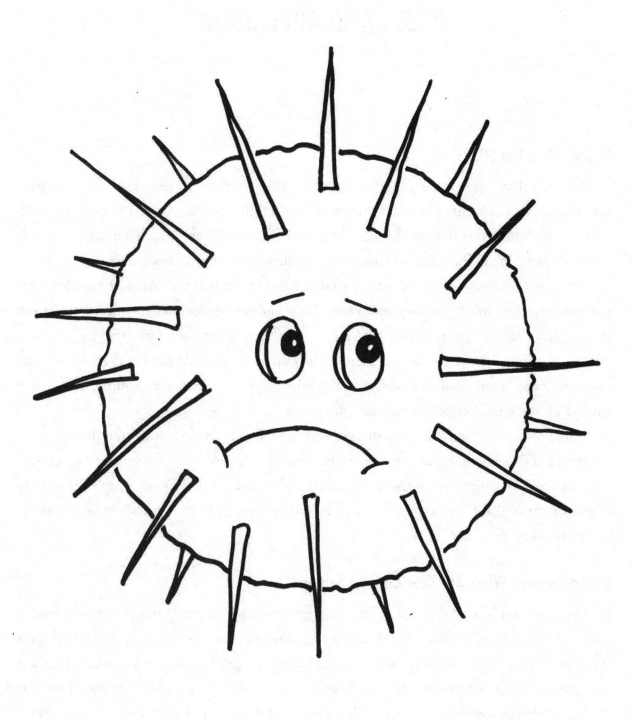

Lesson 7

DRESS AND APPEARANCE

Story: "Are You LDS?"

Tell the following true story. A group of choir students from American Fork, Utah, were traveling in New York City. On Sunday morning many of the students walked through the hotel lobby to board the bus that would take them to a local ward for Church services. A young woman was sitting in the lobby wearing a modest dress. She approached the group.

"Are you LDS?" she asked. When the students responded that they were, she smiled. "Are you going to church?" Again they answered, "Yes." The young woman explained that she was from another state and was traveling with her school sports team. She was the only member of the Church on her team. That morning she had prayed she would be able to find some way to attend church. She had gone down to the lobby to wait. When the group of LDS youth walked in, she knew her prayer had been answered.

After you have shared this story, discuss with your family the following questions:

How did this young woman know that the students she saw were members of The Church of Jesus Christ of Latter-day Saints? Was it how they were dressed? How do people throughout the world know that the young men and women they see are Mormon missionaries? What do our clothes say about us?

Object Lesson: What Are Your Clothes Saying?

Have the family look through several contemporary magazines. Find pictures of models and try to describe what their clothes are saying about each one. Many of the models in these types of magazines are dressed immodestly. What messages are we sending when we dress immodestly? Possible messages include: "I don't respect my body as a sacred gift from Heavenly Father." "I don't know what the prophet has said about modesty or I don't care." "I want you to notice my body first before anything else."

Point out that the person dressing immodestly isn't bad; they just haven't been taught about the importance of modesty or don't understand what their clothes are saying about them. Dressing immodestly can also make other people feel uncomfortable and embarrassed. When someone dresses immodestly, it is hard to notice anything but the person's clothes.

For the Strength of Youth

Read about dress and appearance standards in the *For the Strength of Youth* booklet. Then divide a piece of paper into two columns, one column labeled "Yes" and the other column labeled "No." Write or draw a picture of the things that we should wear on the "Yes" side and the things that we shouldn't wear on the "No" side. Read 1 Corinthians 3:16–17 and Alma 1:27.

Activity: Fashion Show

Read Mosiah 18:9, focusing on the phrase "stand as witnesses of God at all times and in all things, and in all places." We can stand as witnesses by how we dress. We can stand out from the world and be different by our modest clothing.

Have the family imagine they are in a foreign country and want to meet other members of The Church of Jesus Christ of Latter-day Saints. They can't speak the language, so how could they dress to let others know that they are Mormons? Send each family member to his or her bedroom to change clothes and then stage a fashion show.

The fashion show is even more fun if you hang a piece of fabric across the entrance into the family room and let each "model" enter the room by pushing aside the curtain. Try to guess what identifying articles of clothing family members are wearing. Is someone modeling a CTR ring or a Young Women medallion or an angel Moroni tie tack? Is everyone modest? Are we trying to represent the Church and the Savior as we get dressed every day?

Commitment

Encourage family members to always dress modestly and wear clothes that show that they are daughters or sons of God. Remind the children that their bodies are temples and need to be treated with respect. You may want to talk briefly about the temple garment and the importance of preparing now, while they are young, to wear the temple garment when they are older.

Bear your testimony that dressing modestly is important. When we dress modestly, we show others that we love Heavenly Father and that we are following the prophet. We may not always be able to dress in style and we may have to work harder to find modest clothing, but Heavenly Father is pleased with us when we make sacrifices and are different from the crowd.

You may want to have younger family members place a sticker or draw a smiley face on page 16 in the *For the Strength of Youth* booklet. Older family members could choose to write their feelings about their commitment to dress modestly in the booklet or in their journals.

Treat: Out-of-Control Popcorn

Take down the sheet used for the fashion show and lay it on the family room floor. Place a popcorn popper in the center with the lid off. An old fashioned oil popper works best, but an air popper will also work. Have the family sit around the edges of the sheet with bowls and watch the popcorn fly. After the popcorn has landed on the sheet and cooled slightly, the family can gather it up into their bowls and munch away. (I remember doing this as a child and watching delightedly as the popcorn began to pop everywhere!)

Just as we can't control where the popcorn lands, we also can't control what people think of us when we wear immodest clothes.

Lesson 8

ENTERTAINMENT AND THE MEDIA

Story: Bugs, Bugs, Bugs

Tell the story "Bugs, Bugs, Bugs." Talk about the "bugs" or "yucky stuff" that can be in movies, on TV, or on the computer and how we can avoid these things. Use a pair of binoculars, if you would like, for a visual aid.

Bugs, Bugs, Bugs

Dustin had been waiting all week for Saturday, and now it was finally here. Today was the day for a special father-son hike up Silver Creek Canyon. Dustin had been given some binoculars for his birthday the week before and he couldn't wait to try them out.

The drive to Silver Creek seemed to take forever, but finally Dad and Dustin were unloading their packs, lacing up their hiking boots, and starting up the trail. Dustin could hardly keep from racing down the path into the trees. "Hurry, Dad. Come on," Dustin called as he reached the first fork in the trail.

"What's the hurry, son?" Dad asked.

"I don't want to miss any squirrels or birds or rabbits, Dad. This part of the trail just has worms and stuff. All the cool stuff is closer to the creek."

"Take it easy." Dad chuckled. "If you go running into the woods, you really won't see any creatures. You'll just scare away the animals worth seeing. Take your time and you will be surprised at what you discover."

The first thing Dustin spotted with his binoculars was a bird lying on the trail. From far away, it looked like something was moving on the bird's body. When Dustin got closer, he saw that the bird was dead and that it was covered with bugs. "Gross," said Dustin, and he and his father quickly moved down the trail without touching the bird.

41

The second thing Dustin spotted with his binoculars was a log that had fallen across the road. From far away it looked like it had black bark, but up close Dustin could see that the rotting log was covered with bugs. "Sick," said Dustin, as he and his dad skirted the tree and continued down the path.

The third thing Dustin spotted with his binoculars was a man riding a horse ahead of them on the trail to Silver Creek. The horse left behind some droppings that Dustin saw in his binoculars too. "Yuck," said Dustin as they got closer. Flies were swarming all around the horse poop.

"I think the only things I am going to see on this trip are bugs," said Dustin. "Bugs, bugs, bugs! Why do bugs like such gross stuff, Dad?"

"Some types of bugs are attracted to smelly, decaying, and dirty things," said Dad. "I have to admit it isn't the prettiest thing to look at. Keep trying. Those binoculars were made to see more worthwhile things than that."

The next thing that Dustin spotted was a flying squirrel as it jumped from one branch to another. Dustin could see the squirrel's little arms stretched out between the folds of skin that helped him glide from one tree to the next. Dad missed everything because it happened so fast, but Dustin had his binoculars trained on the tree at just the right moment. "Dad, that was the coolest!" Dustin shouted excitedly. "I saw everything!"

Dustin was still talking about the squirrel when he and Dad arrived home from their hike. He couldn't wait to tell Mom about his awesome binoculars. But Mom and the rest of the family were running some errands, so Dad and Dustin walked into the family room and turned on the TV. Instantly, the screen was filled with violence and guns. Dustin knew it wasn't the kind of show they watched in their family. It was worse than seeing the dead bird, the rotting log, or the horse poop on the trail. Dustin quickly picked up his binoculars and said, "Dad, I think I can see bugs all over the TV."

Dad laughed. "You're right, son. This is just the kind of disgusting stuff bugs love." Then Dad quickly turned off the TV, and the two of them went outside to play catch together.

For the Strength of Youth

Read the first, second, and third paragraphs of page 18 in the *For the Strength of Youth* booklet. Read Moroni 7:12–19 and Article of Faith 13. Discuss these standards as a family, then put your knowledge to the test in the following game.

Game: The TV Game

Cut out the TV game cards (see pages 45–47). You will also need a large bowl of gummy worms for this game.

Place the bowl of gummy worms in the center of the table along with the game cards. Each member of the family takes turns picking a card and reading about the TV show it describes. If it is an inappropriate show, you must take two worms out of the bowl and put them on your head. If the card describes a good TV show, you can put back one worm. If you don't have any worms on your head, you can take a worm off another player's head and put it back in the bowl. The game ends when all the cards have been read. The goal is to have no worms on your head. The player with the fewest number of worms on his or her head wins.

Activity: A Fearless Family

Prepare ahead by gathering crayons and drawing paper. For this activity, you can choose to make a roller-box TV or you can simply have the family create the illustrations and hold them up one at a time. If you decide to create a roller-box TV, you will also need to gather a box and some tape, and then follow these instructions:

1. Cut a square in the side of a large box or carton. The opening should be the same size as the pictures to be displayed.

2. Cut two sticks about six inches longer than the width of the box. You might use broom handles, dowel rods, or paper towel tubes.

3. Cut two holes for the sticks at the top and bottom of each side of the box.

4. Insert the sticks through the holes.

5. Give each child a piece of paper, markers or crayons, and instructions on what to draw. Draw the illustrations vertically on the page. The instructions for each page are listed below, letters A through H. You may want to whisper the instructions so the story line remains a secret. You can give some family members two pages to illustrate if you don't have eight members in your family, or you can eliminate some of the illustrations. The only page that cannot be eliminated is letter G.

6. When the pictures are drawn, tape the ends of the pictures together in the proper sequence so they form a single scroll of paper.

7. Attach the bottom end of the scroll to the bottom stick. Roll up the scroll around the stick and attach the top of the scroll to the top stick. Now watch your TV show together by

scrolling through the pictures. Mom or Dad can be the narrator and read the page descriptions below.

    A. Title page: NO FEAR By: Our Family

    B. Our family is not afraid of thunder.

    C. Our family is not afraid of the dark.

    D. Our family is not afraid of monsters.

    E. Our family is not afraid of doctors.

    F. Our family is not afraid of spiders.

    G. Our family is not afraid to walk away from a bad movie or TV show when we know watching it would be wrong.

    H. The end.

Commitment

Read the last paragraph in the section on media on page 19 in the *For the Strength of Youth* booklet. Tell the family about a time when you had the courage to leave a movie, show, or situation that was inappropriate, or talk about a time when you didn't leave but wish that you had. Encourage each family member to make wise choices in the TV shows and movies that they watch as well as in the things that they see on the computer.

Bear your testimony that living this standard can bring powerful blessings into your family's life. You may want to have younger children place a sticker or draw a smiley face on the page for Entertainment and the Media. Older family members could choose to write their feelings about the media and their commitment to follow this standard in the *For the Strength of Youth* booklet or in their journals.

Treat: Dirt Cups with Bugs

Prepare dishes of ice cream or chocolate pudding for each family member. Hide a gummy worm or a plastic insect, such as a fake spider, in each cup. Cover the ice cream or pudding with crushed chocolate cookies to look like dirt. Serve the refreshments and when the bug is discovered, ask this question: If the worm or spider had been real, would you have continued eating? Is it okay to eat dessert if it only has one bug in it? Is it okay to watch a show if it only has one bad part? We shouldn't use that as an excuse for the movies and the shows that we see. Even one bad part can still get in our minds and influence us. Commit as a family to have a "No Bugs" rule for all TV and movie viewing.

When you watch this show, you learn about countries around the world.	This show has characters who disobey their parents and lie to their teachers.	This show has lots of fighting and characters who hit and kick each other.
This movie is R-rated.	This move is G-rated.	This show teaches you how to make a nutritious dinner for your family.
This show has women in it who are dressed immodestly.	This show is about sharing and being kind to your friends.	This show encourages people to drink beer and alcohol.
This show teaches young children the alphabet.	This show is general conference, and the prophet is speaking.	This show causes you to feel happy and good inside.

You would be ashamed if Jesus walked in while you were watching this movie.	This movie tells a scripture story.	This show talks about the importance of good manners.
This movie is PG-rated and your parents haven't said that it is okay for you to watch it.	This show teaches you how to do your family history.	This show makes you want to be good.
This show encourages people to smoke.	This story has a good moral to it and teaches important life lessons.	There are lots of bad words in this show.
The review for this movie said it was very violent.	This is a show that people of all ages would like.	This movie has lots of embarrassing kissing and some nudity.

This show teaches you how to develop your talents.	When you watch this show, you feel grateful for your family.	This show teaches you how to build something.
The Holy Ghost couldn't stay in the room with this movie playing.	This show teaches you how to play a musical instrument.	This movie makes you feel bad inside.
You would feel fine watching this movie with your mom and dad.	This movie teaches good values.	The prophet would like this movie.
This movie doesn't have any bad parts.	You could watch this movie with the Holy Ghost present.	Your friends said there was just one bad part in this movie.

Lesson 9

MUSIC AND DANCING

Story: The Singing Time Day

Give each family member a piece of paper and assign each person one of the following song titles to illustrate: "Quickly, I'll Obey," "A Happy Family," "My Heavenly Father Loves Me," "We Are Different," "When We're Helping," "I'm Trying to Be like Jesus." Then read the story "The Singing Time Day" and hold up the illustrations as Katie sings the songs in the story.

The Singing Time Day

Katie woke up feeling grumpy. She lay in bed, even when Mommy called her down to breakfast. She didn't feel like getting out of bed this morning. Suddenly she heard her daddy coming up the stairs. She thought he would be mad at her, but Daddy was whistling. Katie listened to the tune. Daddy was whistling a Primary song. Katie didn't know that Daddy knew Primary songs, but he was whistling, "Quickly I'll Obey." Katie knew that song. Daddy was whistling for her! Katie jumped out of bed.

"When my Mother calls me, quickly I'll obey," Katie sang as she hopped down the stairs. Already she felt better.

"My goodness," said Mommy. "What happy sounds we have in this house this morning. I love all this whistling and singing."

Daddy looked at Katie and winked. "I'll bet you are going to hear a lot of music in this house today, dear," Daddy said as he smiled and picked up his briefcase for work.

Katie wondered why there was going to be music in the house today. Did Daddy mean that she was going to be singing all day? Maybe she could try it. She already felt happier and she had only sung one song.

After breakfast, Katie began to play house. She tried to get her little brother Daniel to be the baby so that she could be the mommy. But he wouldn't let her hold him or feed him a bottle. Katie started to get mad. Then she remembered that Daddy wanted her to sing.

"I love brother. He loves me. We love Mommy, yessiree. She loves us and so you see. We are a happy family," Katie sang.

Daniel started singing too and soon they were laughing and playing together. Daniel was the dad and Katie was the mom and Katie used a baby-doll to feed instead.

After lunch Mommy and Daniel walked Katie to preschool. On the way, Katie heard a bird singing and saw the daffodils in Mrs. Simpson's yard. Pretty soon she started to sing, "Whenever I hear the song of a bird, or look at the blue, blue sky." Mommy joined in. Soon they were all singing about the "beautiful world Heavenly Father created for me." It was the best walk to preschool Katie had ever had.

At preschool, Katie saw James sitting all by himself, looking sad. She went over and sat by him. She was a little bit embarrassed but she started to sing, "I know you and you know me. We are as different as the sand and the sea." James looked surprised but the song made him smile and soon they were building a castle out of blocks together.

Natalie, Katie's big sister, picked her up at preschool and they walked home together. They hadn't been home long when Mommy asked Natalie to set the table for dinner. Natalie started to moan and groan and complain. Katie jumped up and started to sing, "When we're helping, we're happy and we sing as we go." Then she pulled a chair over to the cupboard and got out the plates. Natalie started to hum along and got out the silverware and glasses.

When Daddy came home, Mommy told him all about Katie's singing and how it had made the family feel so happy. When Daddy tucked Katie into bed that night, he was humming again. Katie snuggled down in bed and listened to Daddy's tune. He was humming, "I'm trying to be like Jesus." Was that what Katie had been doing all day? Being like Jesus? Katie smiled. Singing in Primary always made her happy and helped her to feel close to Heavenly Father and Jesus. She was happy to know that she could have Primary singing time every day.

Object Lesson: Music on the Radio

We are affected by music just like Katie was in the story. We can be affected in negative ways or in positive ways. Even animals and plants can be affected by music. Some plants grow bigger when beautiful music is played nearby. Some animals will move closer to soothing music and run away from loud, pounding music.

Turn on a radio and start scanning through the stations. Have family members pretend that they are an animal like a dog or a cat. They can sneak closer to the radio when they hear beautiful, uplifting music, and they can hide behind the couch or run away when they hear music that is loud with negative lyrics or a pounding beat.

Music has a powerful effect on our emotions and on our spirits. Satan tries to use music to influence us in a negative way. Heavenly Father also uses music to influence us. Singing hymns and Primary songs can help us feel reverent, teach us gospel principles, and bring us closer to Heavenly Father.

For the Strength of Youth

Read the first two paragraphs under "Music and Dancing" on page 20 of the *For the Strength of Youth* booklet. Emphasize that it is important for us to listen to good music. It isn't just a matter of preference; it isn't even the older generation's taste versus the younger generation's taste. It is the Lord's standard. Encourage the family to make good choices in what they listen to. If you have teenagers, also read the last paragraph that talks specifically about dancing. Read Doctrine and Covenants 136:28 and Doctrine and Covenants 25:12.

Activity: Name That Tune

Play "Name That Tune." Divide into two teams. Position the teams where they can't see the music being played. If you have a piano, open the *Children's Songbook* and play the first three notes of a song. The members of Team One try to guess the song from those three notes. If they can't get it, play additional notes until the team can guess the correct song. The team gets the same number of points as the number of notes it took to guess the song. For example, six notes equals six points. Then it is Team Two's turn.

The team with the lowest number of points at the end of a predetermined time or a predetermined number of songs wins. If you don't have a piano, you can hum a few notes of a Primary song or play a few notes from the *Children's Songbook* on tape or CD.

Commitment

Bear your testimony about the importance of listening to good music. You may want to have younger children place a sticker or draw a smiley face on page 21 in the *For the Strength of Youth* booklet. Older family members could choose to write their feelings about music and their commitment to listen to uplifting and positive things in the booklet or in their journals.

Treat: Smoothie Symphony

Make a "Smoothie Symphony." Mix up your favorite smoothie recipe or create a new one by blending together a fruit, a type of juice, and some yogurt or ice cream. Add ice if necessary for a thicker consistency. Pour the smoothie into glass tumblers at different heights and give each family member a spoon. Choose someone to be the conductor, then make music by tapping on the glass rims when the conductor points to you.

Lesson 10

LANGUAGE

Story: I Scream and Salt

Prepare ahead by getting a spoonful of dirt from the backyard and a plateful of salt.

Tell the story "I Scream and Salt." You may want to pause in the middle of the story to teach the object lesson "Dirt in the Salt."

I Scream and Salt

It was a hot day and the family had been working hard picking strawberries from the garden and weeding. Dad knew that nothing would taste better on such a hot day than a bowl of cold homemade strawberry ice cream. Dad pulled out the ice cream freezer from the garage.

He was just going to get the salt and the ice when he heard someone screaming. Josh and Becca were in the backyard, fighting over a swing. Dad moved toward their angry voices. Suddenly he heard Becca yell, "Leave me alone. I hate you!" Josh answered, "Well, you can just go to hell!" The screaming stopped when Dad appeared around the corner of the garage. Both of the children looked at Dad fearfully, wondering what he was going to do.

Dad said quietly, "Becca and Josh, come with me. I need your help with something." The two children followed Dad into the kitchen. Dad still didn't say anything. He grabbed the big silver container filled with milk and sugar and strawberries. He asked Josh to carry the rock salt and the ice and sent Becca to get his scriptures.

Out in the garage Dad put the silver container in the ice cream freezer and attached the motor. Then he turned to the children. "Doesn't strawberry ice cream sound good right now?"

"Yes!" agreed Becca and Josh excitedly.

"Did you know that we can't make ice cream without salt?" Dad asked. The children shook their heads. Ice cream was sweet, not salty. What did Dad mean?

"Salt helps the container stay cold enough to freeze the ice cream." Dad packed the freezer with ice and salt. Then he turned on the motor and motioned for the kids to join him on the porch steps. "Let me tell you kids something about salt. Salt is wonderful for lots of things. It helps to preserve food so it doesn't go bad. It helps to flavor food so that it is delicious to eat. It is a necessary mineral to keep our bodies healthy and functioning properly."

"And it makes ice cream," said Becca.

"And it makes ice cream," said Dad. "Did you know that Jesus compared *us* to salt?" Josh and Becca shook their heads. Dad opened his scriptures to Matthew 5:13. "Listen to what Jesus said. 'Ye are the salt of the earth: but if the salt have lost his savour, wherewith shall it be salted? it is thenceforth good for nothing, but to be cast out, and to be trodden under foot of men.'" Dad closed his scriptures and poured some salt into his hand. "This salt right here is clean and good. It can be used for many things. But what would happen if I did this?" Dad grabbed a handful of dirt from the flower bed beside the porch and mixed the salt and dirt together. "Now could you put this salt on your steak or potatoes? Would you want to eat it or pack it in the ice cream freezer?"

Pause in the story to teach the object lesson "Dirt in the Salt."

Becca and Josh looked at the dirty salt in Dad's hands. "No way!" they said.

"This is what Jesus meant when he said the salt had lost its savour. It can't be used for anything and is only good to trample underfoot. When I came out earlier I heard you two using some very dirty words. Josh said a swear word and Becca said some mean and hurtful words to her brother. When you say those kind of words, it is like mixing dirt in with the salt. Dirty words and stories get in your mind and make it hard for you to think about Jesus. When you say dirty words it makes it hard for you to be a good example to your friends and teach them about the Savior. Just like this salt, you aren't able to do the things that Heavenly Father wants you to do."

Becca and Josh sat quietly thinking about what Dad had said. Dad brushed the dirt and the salt off his hand onto the ground. "I am disappointed in both of you. But I hope that now that you know what those dirty words do to you, you won't use them again." Josh and Becca nodded. Just then the motor on the ice cream freezer stopped making noise.

"Come on," said Dad. "Let's go get some of that yummy strawberry ice cream. I think it's ready."

"Yeah," said Josh. "Thanks to the salt!"

Object Lesson: Dirt in the Salt

Illustrate the effect that dirt has on salt by pouring some table salt on a plate and passing it around the circle and having family members take a little taste with their finger. Then dump a spoonful of dirt onto the salt and mix it up. Ask the family members to take another taste.

After the story is finished, discuss the lesson the dad taught the children. How is using improper language like dumping dirt in the salt? Why is the salt no longer useful? What does using dirty words or telling dirty stories make us unable to do? Possible ideas and answers: we can't be witnesses for Christ; we can't keep our thoughts clean and pure; we can't be good missionaries; we can't have a temple recommend. Encourage the family to come up with additional ideas.

For the Strength of Youth

Read the section on language on pages 22–23 of the *For the Strength of Youth* booklet. Talk about what the prophet expects of us when it comes to language. Read Ephesians 4:29 and James 3:2–13.

Game: Treasure or Trash?

Setup: For this game you will need to copy the Language Game Cards (see page 56). Place a small, clean trash can at one end of the living room with a sign "Words to Trash" taped on the front. Next to the trash can place an open box with a sign "Words to Treasure" taped on the front. At the other end of the family room place the game cards in a pile on a table or chair.

Play: Each family member takes a turn choosing a card from the game pile, reading what it says, and then running across the room to place the card in the appropriate place. If the card says something positive and uplifting, place the card in the "Words to Treasure" box. If the card says something negative or inappropriate, it should go in the trash can. The family member races back to the beginning and touches the hand of the next person in line, who will read the next card. Continue until all the cards have been played.

As a family, review the words in each box. Talk about how those words make you feel.

Commitment

Encourage the family to only say and listen to good things. Language can lift us up and make us better, or it can bring us down and harm our spirits. Bad words can get into our minds and are hard to get out. Sometimes it is impossible to avoid hearing a bad word. If a bad word or thought enters our minds, we can hum a Primary song or hymn to control our thoughts and help us feel better. Controlling our thoughts and only saying good words helps us to be like Jesus and helps us accomplish our mission on the earth. Bear your testimony of this standard.

You may want to have younger children attach a sticker or draw a smiley face on page 23 in the *For the Strength of Youth* booklet. Older family members could choose to write their feelings about language and their commitment to use good language in the booklet or in their journals.

Treat: Ice Cream in a Bag

Make vanilla ice cream in a bag. For each family member, fill a pint-size zip-top plastic bag with 2 tablespoons sugar, 1 cup half-and-half, and 2 teaspoons vanilla. Seal the bag closed with duct tape. Fill a gallon-size zip-top plastic bag with ice and rock salt. Place the pint-sized bag into the gallon-size bag and seal it closed with duct tape as well. Have the family members toss, wiggle, and smash their individual ice cream bags for five minutes. While the children are smashing their bags, talk about the importance of keeping ourselves clean and pure. Ask family members if they would like to mix a scoop of dirt into their bag along with the ice cream. When the ice cream has set up, pull out the pint-size zip-top bag, wipe off the ice and rock salt, and cut off one corner of the bag. Squeeze the ice cream into a bowl and enjoy!

Please	Swear Words	I Love You
You're Welcome	Stupid	You Look Nice
Thank You	The Lord's Name in Vain	Excuse Me
Can I Help?	I Hate You	Heavenly Father's Name Used Reverently in Prayer
Shut Up	Leave Me Alone	I'll Do It

Lesson 11

DATING AND SEXUAL PURITY

Activity: Saving Lives

Prepare ahead by making copies of the boy and girl patients (see pages 61 and 63). Copy and cut out the wedding clothes for the boy and the girl (see pages 62 and 64). Cut out the good and bad word strips for patients (see page 60). Place the good word strips in an envelope. Tape the bad word strips on the applicable part of the patients' bodies. For example, place the word strip "Think Bad Thoughts" on the patient's head. Each patient should be suffering from five bad word strips. For added fun, gather medical supplies to enhance the role-play of the operation. Don rubber gloves when it is your turn to be the surgeon. If you have a play stethoscope or other doctor equipment such as a surgical mask, place these in a bag you have labeled "Dr. Kit."

Begin by telling the family that they get to be doctors. Some of their patients are in serious trouble and they will need to perform life-saving operations to help them. The purpose of the operation is to correct all the things that are wrong with these patients so that they can be married in the temple.

Have each family member take a turn being the doctor. Put on the doctor gear and remove the wrong actions from the patients, replacing them with the right actions. Have family members guess what the correct behavior would be in each situation. Then the surgeon can find the correct strip in the envelope. Discuss with the family why the bad behavior would keep the patient out of the temple. Emphasize that even small things can have big consequences, and correcting these little things now can make a difference later on.

Place the good action strips on the borders of the page rather than directly on the patient. This will give you room to put the wedding clothes on the patient at the end of the activity.

Ailment	Replace...	With...
Headache	Think Bad Thoughts	Have Good Thoughts
Poor Eyesight	Look at Pornography and Bad Movies	Only Watch Good and Uplifting Things
Deaf Ears	Ignore Parents	Listen to Parents
Illness of the Mouth	Swear and Talk Dirty	Speak like a Child of God
Pulled Shoulder	Hang Out with Bad Friends	Stand Close to Good Friends
Broken Heart	Act Immorally	Stay Morally Clean
Sick Stomach	Drink, Smoke, and Take Drugs	Live the Word of Wisdom
Dirty Hands	Read Dirty Books	Read the Scriptures
Cramped Legs	Wear Immodest Clothing	Dress Modestly
Stiff Knees	Never Pray	Pray Often
Lost Feet	Walk in the Ways of the World	Follow Jesus Christ

After all the changes have been made, tell the family that this really was a life-and-death situation. The patient's *spiritual* life was at stake. Without the operations they would have spiritually died and they would not have been able to be with an eternal family forever. But now they are ready to go to the temple. Put the temple wedding dress and the tuxedo on the patients. Bear your testimony of the importance of staying morally clean.

For the Strength of Youth

Read what the prophet has said about dating on pages 24–25 of the *For the Strength of Youth* booklet. Explain that even though the children aren't old enough to date, they should learn these standards now so that they will be prepared to live them later on. By following these standards, they will be ready and worthy to marry their eternal companion in the house of the Lord.

Read 2 Corinthians 6:14 and Doctrine and Covenants 38:42. You may also want to share the story of Joseph of Egypt and Potiphar's wife found in Genesis 39:1–12.

Depending on the ages of your children, you may choose to read some paragraphs from the section on sexual purity found on pages 26–27. If you don't want to discuss this section, say something like, "This section is for teenagers and we will talk about this when you are older." For older children and pre-teenagers you may wish to say something like the following: "When a mother and father love each other and have a baby together that is called sex or physical intimacy. It is a wonderful thing when a mother and a father bring a new baby into this world. It is a special gift from God. But Satan says it is okay to have sex and have a baby when you are not married. Heavenly Father has taught us this is wrong." The first three paragraphs on page 26 explain this principle and can be used without a full "birds-and-the-bees" discussion. Prayerfully consider how much to present to your family.

Commitment

Conclude by bearing your testimony of the importance of staying morally clean. A parent may wish to share his or her feelings about his or her spouse, dating experiences, or temple marriage. Share the blessings that have come as a result of living this important standard.

You may want to have younger children place a sticker or draw a smiley face on page 25 in the *For the Strength of Youth* booklet. Older family members could choose to write their feelings about these principles and their commitment to remain morally clean in the booklet or in their journals.

Treat: All-White Dessert

Serve an all-white dessert and talk about the importance of staying pure and clean. Ideas include a slice of angel food cake topped with vanilla ice cream, whipped cream, and white chocolate chips.

Think Bad Thoughts	Stay Morally Clean
Have Good Thoughts	Drink, Smoke, and Take Drugs
Look at Bad Movies and Pornography	Live the Word of Wisdom
Only Watch Good and Uplifting Things	Read Dirty Books
Ignore Parents	Read the Scriptures
Listen to Parents	Wear Immodest Clothing
Swear and Talk Dirty	Dress Modestly
Speak like a Child of God	Never Pray
Hang Out with Bad Friends	Pray Often
Stand Close to Good Friends	Walk in the Ways of the World
Act Immorally	Follow Jesus Christ

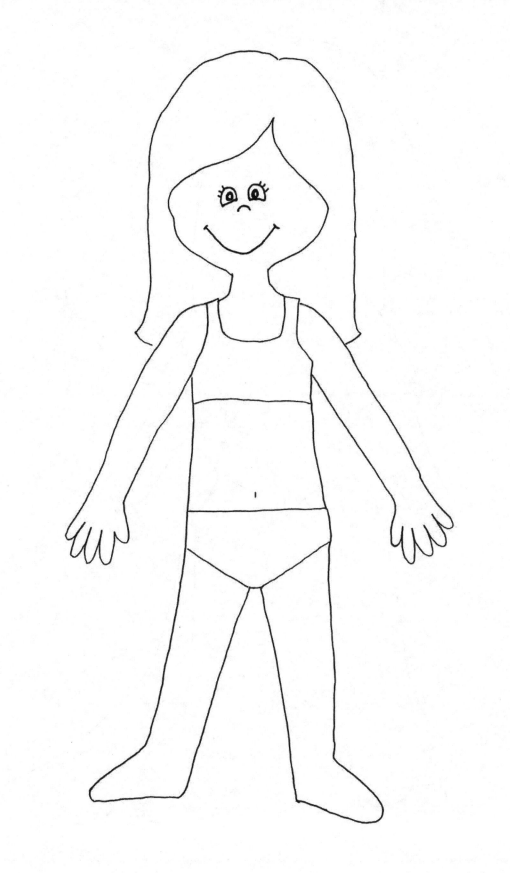

Lesson 12

REPENTANCE

Activity: Fixing the Car

Have Dad or another family member read this section and be prepared to drive "the car." Arrange kitchen chairs in the living room in rows to simulate a car. Use a large mixing bowl as a steering wheel.

Begin by asking the family to go on a drive in a new car. Seat the family on the kitchen chairs. Dad (or another family member prepared ahead of time) sits in the driver's seat and holds the steering wheel (mixing bowl). He drives the family on their adventure. The trip starts out smoothly, but soon problems start to appear. Dad dramatically describes all the things that start going wrong with the car (the brakes go out, the steering wheel breaks off, the tires go flat, the engine starts smoking, etc.). The sillier and more outrageous the driver acts, the better. Lead the rest of the family in begging Dad to pull over the car before he gets in an accident. He refuses. He insists that the car doesn't need to be fixed. The gas pedal still works and that is all he needs. Eventually, Dad pretends to crash and bodies and chairs fall all over the living room.

When the family is calm and sitting down, ask the following question: Would Dad really do that in a real car? No, he wouldn't. When anything goes wrong with the car, he stops immediately and gets it fixed. He either finds the tools and fixes it himself or finds someone else who can fix it. Dad keeps the car in good repair because he wants us to be safe and to have an enjoyable trip in the car.

Fixing the car is a lot like repentance. When we make mistakes and things get broken in our lives, we need to stop and repent before things can be fixed and run smoothly again. Can a car be fixed on its own? Will the problems in the car just go away if we ignore the problems or simply continue to drive the car? No. It is the same with our lives. Our mistakes and problems won't just go away either. Because of Jesus Christ and his atonement, we have all the tools that we need to fix our mistakes and make our lives run smoothly again.

Story: More Than Soccer Stains

Tell the story "More Than Soccer Stains." A Butterfinger candy bar and a soccer shirt would make great visual aids as you tell the story. Discuss the consequences of stealing and how it was important for Jake to stop and repent.

More Than Soccer Stains

Jake really wanted a Butterfinger candy bar. His soccer team had just won a big game and Jake had run up and down the field hundreds of times. He was hungry and tired, and he knew that a candy bar would taste good. On the way home from the game, they stopped at the store for a few groceries. But Mom had already said that Jake couldn't get a candy bar this time because it would spoil his lunch.

Jake looked around. No one was over by the candy bar racks. Mom was up front paying for the groceries. He could slip a Butterfinger into his jacket pocket and no one would even know about it. Jake's heart started racing and his hands felt sweaty as he quickly grabbed the Butterfinger off the shelf and put it in his pocket. He looked around nervously and headed to the front of the store with his mom.

Jake couldn't get out of the store fast enough. He felt scared even as Mom started driving away. When they got home, Jake didn't help his mom carry in the groceries like he normally did. He just ran up to his room and closed the door. Sitting on the floor, Jake pulled the candy bar out of his jacket pocket. He quickly unwrapped it and shoved the whole thing in his mouth.

Jake chewed and swallowed as fast as he could and then shoved the candy wrapper under his bed as far as he could reach. Jake was surprised that the Butterfinger didn't really taste all that good and after it was gone, he felt a little bit sick inside.

"Jake!" Mom was calling him down to lunch. Jake brushed his hands off on his soccer shorts and then looked down at his soccer shirt. Oh no! There was a huge chocolate stain right on the name of his team. Some chocolate must have dripped out of Jake's mouth when he stuffed it so full. Jake hurried to change and shoved the soccer shirt under the bed with the rest of the evidence.

All day Jake felt funny, and when he went to bed that night he didn't feel like saying his prayers. He didn't feel like listening in Primary the next day when they talked about being honest. He kept whispering and bothering other people until his teacher got upset. Monday he forgot to say his prayers again. Every day it got easier and easier to forget about what he had done

66

on Saturday. He started to think that it didn't really matter anymore. Then Saturday came and it was time to get ready for his next soccer game.

When Jake went to find his soccer uniform it wasn't in his drawer where his mom usually put it. Mom said that she hadn't seen it in the laundry room. Then Jake remembered his shirt was under his bed. When he dug out the shirt, the chocolate stain looked worse than he remembered. It was dark brown and covered the name of his team so he couldn't even read it. Coach made a big deal about coming to the games looking like a winning team. Jake would look like a loser in this dirty and wrinkled shirt. He didn't know what he was going to do.

Jake sat in his room staring at the shirt for a long time, then he took a deep breath and went to find his mom. Mom listened patiently as he poured out the whole story in a rush. She didn't get mad, but pulled him close for a big hug and thanked him for having the courage to tell the truth. They talked about repentance and the things that Jake would need to do to receive forgiveness for his big mistake.

Mom drove Jake to the game and Jake told his coach that he couldn't play today because he had made a big mistake. He apologized to the team and told them he would be there to cheer them on. It was hard to watch the team, especially when they didn't win, but Jake knew he had done the right thing. It was even harder to go to the grocery store with Mom and tell the owner about the stolen candy bar. It was scary, but it felt really good to pay the store back for the candy bar he had taken.

When they got home, Jake helped Mom put stain remover on his soccer shirt. Then he went to his room to pray and ask for forgiveness from Heavenly Father.

When the soccer shirt came out of the wash, Mom came to show Jake the chocolate stain was gone. His shirt looked as good as new.

"Mom," Jake said, "that is just like repentance. I feel clean and good inside again just like my shirt."

Mom smiled and gave Jake another hug. "You are right," she said. "Jesus took away the stain from your spirit, and that is even more important than the stains coming off your soccer shirt. I am so proud of you. How would you like to share this treat with me?"

Jake laughed as Mom pulled a Butterfinger out of her pocket. Mom had paid for this one, and this time it tasted really good.

Object Lesson: Repentance Tool Kit

Gather the tools needed for the object lesson. Create labels to place on each tool (see page 70). Tell the family that you have a repentance tool kit. Display each tool one at a time and discuss what it means. Place the label on each tool so that family members will remember what they mean.

Measuring Tape

"Measure" up to your mistakes. The first step is to recognize that we have done something wrong and to feel remorse for the mistake.

Paintbrush

"Brush" up on these words: "I'm sorry. Please forgive me." The second step is to ask for forgiveness from Heavenly Father and anyone we have hurt.

Hammer

"Handle" the consequences of your mistakes and do your best to make things right. The third step is to make restitution and do what we can to fix our mistakes. This could mean paying to fix a broken window, returning a stolen candy bar, or giving your sister a hug to help her feel better.

Screwdriver

Everyone "screws" up sometimes. Learn from your mistakes and don't repeat them. The fourth step is to become a better person by working to not make the same mistake again.

Saw

God "saw" the need for an atonement. We need to see the importance of it in our own lives. Without repentance, none of us could return to live with Heavenly Father again. Jesus died for us and gave us the opportunity to repent. This is a critical part of Heavenly Father's plan for our lives.

Pliers

"Tighten" up your relationship with Heavenly Father by repenting every day. When we commit sins we move farther and farther away from God. But if we follow the steps of repentance, we can be forgiven and feel close to Heavenly Father and Jesus Christ again. Just as it wouldn't make sense to keep driving a car with bad brakes, it doesn't make sense to hang on to our sins when we can repent and be clean and whole again.

For the Strength of Youth

Read all or part of the section on repentance (pages 29–30) in the *For the Strength of Youth* booklet. Discuss what a blessing the gift of repentance is to us. Testify of the importance of repentance and the great tool it is in our lives. Read Doctrine and Covenants 58:42. You may wish to tell the conversion story of Alma the Younger found in Alma 36:6–24.

Commitment

Bear your testimony of the power and importance of the Atonement and the miracle of repentance. You may want to have younger children place a sticker or draw a smiley face on page 30 in the *For the Strength of Youth* booklet. Older family members could choose to write their feelings about repentance in the booklet or in their journals.

Treat: Butterfinger Angel Cake

You will need 1 angel food cake, 1 large container of Cool Whip, and 1 package bite-size Butterfinger candy bars. Unwrap all the Butterfinger candy bars and put them in a plastic zip-top bag. Have family members take turns using a hammer to crush the candy bars. Remind the family that we all need to "handle" our mistakes with repentance. It takes the Savior to put our lives back together again. Mix the crushed candy bars into the Cool Whip and spread evenly over the entire angel food cake. Cut and serve.

Labels for Tools

"Measure" up to your mistakes.	Everyone "screws" up sometimes. Learn from your mistakes and don't repeat them.
"Brush" up on these words: "I'm sorry. Please forgive me."	God "saw" the need for an atonement. We need to see the importance of it in our own lives.
"Handle" the consequences of your mistakes and do your best to make things right.	"Tighten" up your relationship with your Heavenly Father by repenting every day.

HONESTY

Activity: Honesty Heroes

Prepare ahead for this activity by talking privately to a few family members about a time when they were honest. Copy the Honesty Awards (see page 74).

Set up some chairs in the living room to resemble a talk show stage. Using a large spoon or spatula as a microphone, act like your favorite talk show host as you tell the family that there are some heroes in the house. These heroes had great courage and did something that many people in the world can't do. Ask one family member to sit on the chair in front. Introduce this person as your first hero. What did this person do to become a hero? He or she was honest. Dramatically interview this person. What was the story? What were the consequences? How did it make this person feel? At the end of the interview, have the rest of the family clap for this hero. Interview as many family members as you can. Hand out the Honesty Awards. Make a big fuss over these special guests!

Story: Joseph Smith and the First Vision

It takes great courage to tell the truth. Even as a young man, the Prophet Joseph Smith had great courage and always told the truth—even when some of the adults around him wanted him to lie. Tell the story of Joseph Smith and the First Vision as well as some of the events that occurred after the First Vision. Joseph's family believed him, but many others didn't. Read Joseph Smith–History 1:24–25. Even when adults came to Joseph and told him to lie and deny the things he had seen, he still told the truth. He was beaten and persecuted for telling the truth, and he was still honest. Joseph Smith was a great hero, and we can look up to him and follow his example. Even when people around us don't know we are lying, we need to remember that Heavenly Father knows the truth and we can't hide our actions from him.

For the Strength of Youth

Read what the prophet says about honesty on page 31 in the *For the Strength of Youth* booklet. Read Exodus 20:15–16 and Alma 27:27.

Discussion

Read the six scenarios and ask family members to respond with the correct action for each situation.

1. Stephanie went grocery shopping with her mom. While she was at the store, she saw a candy bar that she really wanted. Stephanie didn't have any money. She put the candy bar in her pocket anyway. Was this honest? What should Stephanie do?

2. Jason wanted to go to the school football game with his friends. His mom said he couldn't go to the game, but could go to a Church activity instead. Jason agreed, but when he left the house, he went to the football game instead of the Church activity. Was this honest? What should Jason do?

3. Megan was having a hard time in her math class at school. The final exam was coming quickly and she hadn't studied for it. Her best friend, Lisa, said Megan could look at her answers during the test. Is Megan being honest? Is Lisa being honest? What should they do?

4. Amy told her best friend, Melissa, a personal secret. Melissa promised not to tell anyone. When Amy wasn't around, Melissa told Amy's secret to others. Was this honest? What should Melissa do?

5. Cory and Daniel were good friends at school. Cory always talked about the pets he had at home. Daniel doesn't have any pets, but he told Cory he has a dog and talked about his dog all the time. Is this honest? What should Daniel do?

6. Matthew used Dad's tools to try to fix his bike, then he left them out. When Dad got home, he couldn't find his tools and asked if anyone had seen them. Matthew didn't say anything. Is this honest? What should Matthew do?

Game: Sneaky Snakes

This tag game is called Sneaky Snakes. One of Satan's names is "that old serpent" (D&C 76:28) and another of his names is "the father of . . . lies" (Moses 5:24). This game can help us remember to avoid being sneaky and dishonest like a snake.

Begin by designating the boundaries of the play area, not too large or too small. One person is chosen to be "It." He chases the other family members around the designated playing area. When he tags another person, that person becomes a snake. Once you become a snake, you must lay down on the ground where you were tagged and move your arms and legs back and forth to wiggle across the floor trying to tag other players. The players must run from "It" as well as avoid being tagged by the wiggling snake. When someone else is tagged by "It" or by a snake, he or she becomes another snake to help catch the other players. The last person left standing is the winner. He or she becomes "It" for the next round.

Commitment

Satan is constantly tempting us to be dishonest. Each time we tell the truth, we become stronger and more able to withstand the temptation to lie. But each time we lie, we become weaker and more easily influenced by Satan. It is important to always tell the truth. It takes courage, but it will bring great blessings. Bear your testimony of the principle of honesty.

You may want to have younger children place a sticker or draw a smiley face on page 31 in the *For the Strength of Youth* booklet. Older family members could choose to write their feelings about honesty and their commitment to be more honest in the booklet or in their journals.

Treat: Cinnamon Roll Snake

Buy the packaged cinnamon roll dough that comes in a can. Arrange the cinnamon rolls on a cookie sheet in the shape of a snake. Bake your snake according to the package directions. Tint the frosting with food coloring and frost the snake with a diamond-shaped pattern on its back. After the cinnamon roll snake has cooled, add a fruit roll-up tongue and chocolate chip eyes. Remind the family to be honest and to resist the temptation to lie from the sneaky snake, Satan.

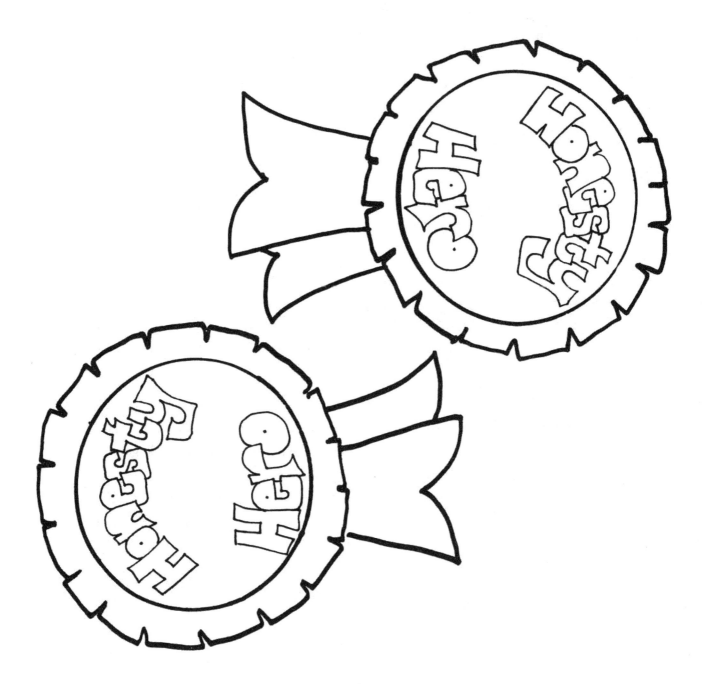

HONESTY AWARDS

Lesson 14

SABBATH DAY OBSERVANCE

Story: Sunday Sam

Copy and color the picture of Sunday Sam the mouse (see page 79). Then gather the following items to use as visual aids for the story: a basketball, a garden trowel or small shovel, keys, dollar bills, a cable for the TV or VCR, and a sock.

Tell the story "Sunday Sam" about a mouse who keeps the Sabbath day holy. Use the mouse figure and the objects you have collected around the house to tell the story.

Sunday Sam

My name is Sam, but everyone calls me Sunday Sam because ever since I was really little, I have loved doing what is right on Sunday.

Show the picture of the mouse.

Mom says that I keep the Sabbath day holy. But the human people we live with don't. At least they go to church on Sunday morning. I usually hitch a ride with Steve.

If you would like, have Dad wear a Sunday shirt and put the mouse in the front pocket.

But when they get home, Steve and the rest of the family act like it is a regular day. Once Steve and his brother began to wrestle and fight on the kitchen floor. I stood on Steve's head and shouted, "It is Jesus' special day and he can hear you!" But no one even heard me.

Take the mouse out of Dad's pocket.

One Sunday Steve started to play basketball until I ended the game early by biting a hole in the ball.

Show the basketball.

Another Sunday Steve's mom started to wash the laundry, so I hid in the dirty clothes. When she saw me and started to scream . . . well, that ended *that* activity for awhile.

Place the sock over Sam.

One Sunday Steve's dad wanted to work in the garden, but I got to the garden first and buried the tools.

Put the garden trowel or small shovel behind Sam.

Once Steve's brother was watching a bad show on TV. I had to stop him, too.

Hide the cable behind Sam.

Almost every Sunday the family goes to the store or out to eat, but I know how to keep them from buying anything. You can't get very far without money.

Put the dollar bill behind Sam's back.

I even figured out a way to keep the family from going boating on Sundays.

Put the key behind Sam's back.

If only I could help them see how much happier they would be if they did the things Jesus wanted them to do.

On Sundays I love to read about the mice in the Bible. I like to feast on the words in the Book of Mormon. I like to take cookie crumbs to the widow mouse in the house next door. Sometimes I visit my sick Grandma Mouse and sing her my favorite Primary songs. I love to write letters to my big brother, Missionary Mouse, and I love to think about Jesus.

If Steve would just keep the Sabbath day holy, I could call him Sunday Steve and stay in his pocket all day. Do you keep the Sabbath day holy? Maybe I could come live with you!

For the Strength of Youth

Read what the prophet has said on pages 32–33 about keeping the Sabbath day holy in the *For the Strength of Youth* booklet.

Make a list of at least ten things the prophet teaches us we should do on the Sabbath day. Then list at least five things that constitute breaking the Sabbath. You may notice there are many more positive things you can do on the Sabbath. Focusing on the good things you can do, instead of on the things you can't do, will help you draw closer to Heavenly Father and make Sunday a special day.

Bear testimony that Heavenly Father blesses those who honor him. When we honor the Sabbath day, we are really honoring God and showing our commitment and love to him. Read Exodus 20:8 and Doctrine and Covenants 59:9–13.

Activity: Scripture Play Dough

This is a fun activity you can do on Sunday to help keep the Sabbath day holy. Make or buy some play dough. Give each member of the family some play dough and then take a few minutes to sculpt something that fits in the first category below. (Example: if the category is the Book of Mormon, a family member might sculpt a bow and arrow for the story of Nephi's broken bow. Older family members can pair up with younger family members who may need help.) Once everyone has finished his or her simple sculpture, the other family members can guess what was made. Sculpt as many categories as you would like or have time for. Save the rest for the next Sunday.

Play Dough Categories

Sculpt something from your favorite story in the Old Testament.

Sculpt something from your favorite story in the New Testament.

Sculpt something from your favorite story in the Book of Mormon.

Sculpt something that Joseph Smith would have used.

Sculpt something that God has given you that you are grateful for.

Sculpt something that you like to do to keep the Sabbath day holy.

Sculpt something that you like to do with your family.

Sculpt something that the pioneers would have used.

Sculpt something that you might see in heaven.

Play Dough Recipe

2 cups water

3 tablespoons oil

Food coloring

2 cups flour

2 cups salt

1 tablespoon alum (Alum is available in the spice section of the grocery store. Cream of tartar can also be used as a substitute.)

Boil the water. Add the oil and food coloring. Remove from heat. Stir in dry ingredients. Mix well and knead until soft. This dough will keep for a month or more if sealed in an airtight container.

Commitment

Bear your testimony about the Sabbath day and how keeping it holy has been a blessing in your life. You may want to have younger children place a sticker or draw a smiley face on page 32 in the *For the Strength of Youth* booklet. Older family members could choose to write their feelings about Sunday and their commitment to keep the Sabbath day holy in the booklet or in their journals.

Treat: Sunday Sundaes

Serve ice cream "Sunday" sundaes. Set out a variety of toppings: M&Ms, nuts, chocolate chips, sprinkles, cherries, etc. Tell the family that the more positive activities they choose to participate in on Sunday, the more "delicious" and wonderful the day will become to them. For each topping added, have family members name one positive thing they can do on Sunday.

SUNDAY SAM

Lesson 15

TITHES AND OFFERINGS

Story: Sunday Sam Pays Tithing

Gather up the following items to use as visual aids for the story: the picture of Sunday Sam the mouse (see page 79), a one-dollar bill, a toy car, a jug of milk, a toaster, a plant, a doll, a computer CD, and a tithing envelope.

Tell the story "Sunday Sam Pays Tithing." If you would like, you can leave the objects such as the milk and the toaster in their proper places and the children can hide the dollar bill in the fridge or the other places as the story progresses.

Sunday Sam Pays Tithing

My name is Sam, but everyone calls me Sunday Sam because ever since I was really little, I have loved doing what is right on Sunday. I like doing what is right on Monday, Tuesday, Wednesday, Thursday, Friday, and Saturday, too. I especially like to pay my tithing.

Show the picture of the mouse.

The human boy that I live with doesn't always like to pay his tithing, but I keep working on him. One day Steve received $10.00 for mowing the neighbor's yard. I was proud of Steve for setting aside $1.00 to pay his tithing. The problem started when he left the dollar bill on his dresser.

Show the $1.00 bill.

A few days later, I was riding in Steve's pocket as he rode his bike to the store. There was the computer game that we wanted to buy: "Mouse Track Speedway." I almost fell out of Steve's pocket I was so excited. Then we saw the price tag. It cost exactly $10.00. I knew that we would have to wait.

But Steve said he had to have the game *right now!* I knew he only had $9.00. That could only mean one thing. As soon as we got home from the store, I took a shortcut through the wall up to his room. I raced to the dresser and grabbed his tithing dollar. I had to hide it, but where?

Show the $1.00 bill.

I hid it in his toy race car and waited quietly in my mouse hole.

Put the dollar behind the toy car.

Steve stomped around his room looking for his money. Then I heard him talking to his mom in the other room. His mom said, "Son, I know you want that computer game, but I don't have the money. Why don't you play with your racetrack instead?"

Yikes! I raced out of the mouse hole and grabbed the dollar bill out of the car just in time. I figured I had better hide it somewhere far away from Steve's room. I quietly carried the dollar bill all the way downstairs to the kitchen and hid it behind the milk in the fridge.

Put the dollar behind the milk bottle.

I was about to leave the fridge through a secret hole at the bottom when the fridge door opened. I was almost blinded by the light. Steve was looking for a snack! I grabbed the dollar bill and raced down the fridge shelves before Steve could see me. I ran through the tunnel and into a cupboard next to the fridge. Whew! I was safe for now. I carefully hid the tithing money in the toaster.

Put the dollar behind the toaster.

Was that ever a mistake! No sooner had I popped out of the toaster, than I heard Steve yell, "Mom, can I toast a bagel?" Not again! This tithing would soon be toast!

I grabbed the money and ran behind the cupboard and through the wall into the living room. There was one place I knew Steve would never look. The plant! Steve was always getting in trouble because he forgot to water the plants. The tithing money would be safe there.

Put the dollar behind the plant.

I was just catching my breath when I heard Steve's mom yell from upstairs, "Honey, after you're done eating, put the toaster away and water the plants." This was not my lucky day. Serious problems call for serious actions. I knew I would have to take drastic measures, so I hid the tithing money in Susie's doll. Steve would never look there and the tithing money would be safe until Sunday, when we could take it to church.

Put the dollar behind the doll.

I curled up behind the doll, exhausted. I had just fallen asleep when the doll was jerked upwards. I looked up to see Steve standing overhead. "I knew Susie stole my money! She was hiding it in her doll. Now I can go buy that game."

"No, Steve," I squeaked. "That's your tithing money!" But Steve didn't listen to me. He was too busy racing out the door.

A little while later Steve was back. He wanted me to come play "Mouse Track Speedway" with him, but I wouldn't because he had gotten the game by stealing the Lord's money. Steve left the room and I thought he was going to play the game alone, but a few minutes later, he came back in the room with an unopened CD.

Show the computer CD.

I could hardly believe what Steve said to me. "Come on, little buddy. Let's return this game to the store. I don't feel good about taking my tithing money. When I get that dollar back you can help me find a tithing envelope to put it in."

I was so excited I did three flips in Steve's pocket. I found a tithing envelope for him as soon as we got home. Paying tithing makes mice and boys feel good inside.

Put the dollar in the tithing envelope.

For the Strength of Youth

Read what the prophet has said about tithing in the *For the Strength of Youth* booklet. Read the three paragraphs on page 34 and Malachi 3:10. Ask the family what they think it means when God says that he will "open . . . the windows of heaven, and pour . . . out a blessing." Ask the family what kinds of blessings could come to a family that pays a faithful tithe. (Answers could include happiness, success, miracles, help, the Holy Ghost, prosperity, strength to endure challenges, protection, extra power over temptation, eternal rewards, etc.) Ask if any family member wouldn't want these blessings. The amount we have been asked to give the Lord is so small, and he rewards us with so much more in return.

Bear testimony of the power of tithing and share any experiences you have had where you have been blessed for paying your tithing.

Game: Tithing Toss

Copy the Tithing Toss game cards (see pages 84–85) and cut them out. Spread them out facedown on a tile floor or tabletop.

Choose one of Dad's old ties that he doesn't want anymore to be the Tithing Tie and lay it on a piece of newspaper. Spray the wide end of the tie with a little bit of spray glue. (You may need to reapply the glue occasionally during play if the tie loses the stickiness necessary to pick up a card.)

Each family member takes turns throwing out the sticky Tithing Tie, fishing for a card. When the tie snags a card, the player reels in the card and then tells how much tithing is owed on the amount listed. If the player gives the correct amount, he or she gets to keep the card. If the player gives an incorrect answer, he or she must replace the card on the ground.

The player with the most cards at the end wins. For older children, the player whose cards total the highest monetary amount wins. If you do not wish to use a tie, simply lay the cards out facedown and take turns choosing a card and determining the correct amount of tithing.

Commitment

Bear testimony to the family about the importance of tithing. Heavenly Father doesn't need our money, but he does need our obedience; when we pay tithing we are showing our commitment to him. Even when the amount of money earned is very small, we should always pay tithing first.

You may want to have younger children draw a smiley face or put a sticker on page 35 in the *For the Strength of Youth* booklet. Older family members could choose to write their feelings about tithing and their commitment to pay a full tithing in the booklet or in their journals.

Treat: Chocolate Coins

Serve tithing candy. Pass out ten chocolate coins (or another type of individualized treat) to each family member. Ask them to give back one-tenth of that amount. Illustrate how much more they get to keep than they have to give back. Heavenly Father is so generous with us, giving us everything and asking such a small amount in return. Eat the chocolate coins and enjoy!

$4.00	$0.60	$6.35
$10.50	$3.60	$2.00
$1.80	$14.00	$14.10
$5.00	$0.10	$50.00
$100.00	$7.50	$8.00

$5.15	$12.00	$0.55
$9.00	$95.00	$25.00
$18.75	$17.25	$1.00
$7.90	$21.00	$13.00

Lesson 16

PHYSICAL HEALTH

Story: The Courage of Daniel, Shadrach, Meshach, and Abed-nego

Tell the story of Daniel and his three friends, Shadrach, Meshach and Abed-nego from Daniel 1:3–20. Talk about the courage it took for these young men to stand up to the king and to obey the Word of Wisdom. Remind the family about the things that happened to these young men later in their lives. If they hadn't overcome this challenge and been faithful in this small thing, they wouldn't have had the faith to face the lions (Daniel) and the fiery furnace (Shadrach, Meshach, and Abed-nego) in the future. If they had given in and eaten the kings' food and wine, it is likely they would have failed in overcoming these later tests of faith and character.

For the Strength of Youth

Read what the First Presidency has said about the Word of Wisdom in the *For the Strength of Youth* booklet on pages 36–37. Notice the problems that can come from using harmful substances. Next notice the promises that come to those who keep the Lord's commandments. The last paragraph explains some of the lies that Satan uses to get people to break the Word of Wisdom. How does he sell this message? Why do people believe it? One family has the tradition of yelling "It's a trap" every time they see a beer commercial on TV to help them recognize one of the traps that Satan has set.

Read the promises given in the Word of Wisdom found in Doctrine and Covenants 89:18–20. If desired, read the entire section as a family.

Object Lesson: The Raccoon Trap

Copy and color the raccoon mask (see page 89). Tie a piece of yarn to each side of the mask so that it can be tied around a family member's head. Set out some tinfoil.

Explain that one of the worst problems with harmful substances like drugs or alcohol is that they are addictive. People lose the ability to choose and control their own lives when they become addicted to alcohol, cigarettes, or drugs. It is like the story of the raccoons.

Some trappers learned an easy way to trap raccoons. They would simply put a shiny coin or piece of metal in the bottom of a box. Then they would close the box, but leave a small hole on the top. The raccoon would see the metal and reach in through the hole. With his fist closed around the coin, he couldn't get his hand out of the box. All he would have to do is let go of the worthless piece of metal to be free, but the raccoon would refuse to drop the coin. He would stay trapped until he starved to death or was captured. The same is true for those with addictions. They will do anything for their next drink or smoke or drug-induced high, including destroying their own lives and everyone around them.

Demonstrate this by putting the raccoon mask on a family member. Then tie a piece of tinfoil around a doorknob near where the family is. Instruct the "raccoon" to hold tightly to the foil and not let go. Begin to play a fun family game or eat some refreshments in sight of the "raccoon." The raccoon wants to participate but must just watch since he or she can't let go of the foil. Take turns playing the part of the raccoon. Ask the question, "How did being trapped by a worthless piece of foil make you feel?" Help the family compare this to an addiction to drugs or alcohol or tobacco.

Story: A Glass of Milk

One LDS young man was attending an awards banquet where many successful businessmen were being recognized for their achievements. He was honored to be invited to the banquet and wanted to be accepted by his business associates. When the meal was served, wine was poured into each glass. At first the young man thought that he would let the waiter pour the wine and he'd simply leave it on the table. But if there were any toasts at the end of the banquet that would be a problem.

As the waiter moved closer to his table, the young man decided that he would whisper to the waiter that he wanted 7-Up instead of the wine. That way he could participate in the toasts and no one would know the difference. Just as the waiter reached his table, the young man asked himself, *What would the prophet do if he were here?* Thinking about the prophet gave him courage. He ordered milk so that everyone around him would know that he wasn't drinking alcohol. At the end of the banquet, he proudly toasted the winning businessmen with his glass of milk.

Encourage the family to follow this young man's example in having the courage to keep the Word of Wisdom. Share any personal experiences you have had keeping this standard.

Commitment

Bear your testimony of the blessings that have come to you because of your decision to live this standard. You may want to have younger children place a sticker or draw a smiley face on page 37 in the *For the Strength of Youth* booklet. Older family members could choose to write about their commitment to live the Word of Wisdom and not drink, smoke, or take drugs in the booklet or in their journals.

Treat: Milkshakes

Make milkshakes by mixing milk with ice cream and any other syrups, fruits, or jams of your choice. Remember the young man who was proud to drink milk and keep the Word of Wisdom. You could also put a small line of vanilla yogurt on each person's upper lip and take pictures of the family with their "milk moustaches." These silly pictures can remind family members of their commitment to keep the Word of Wisdom.

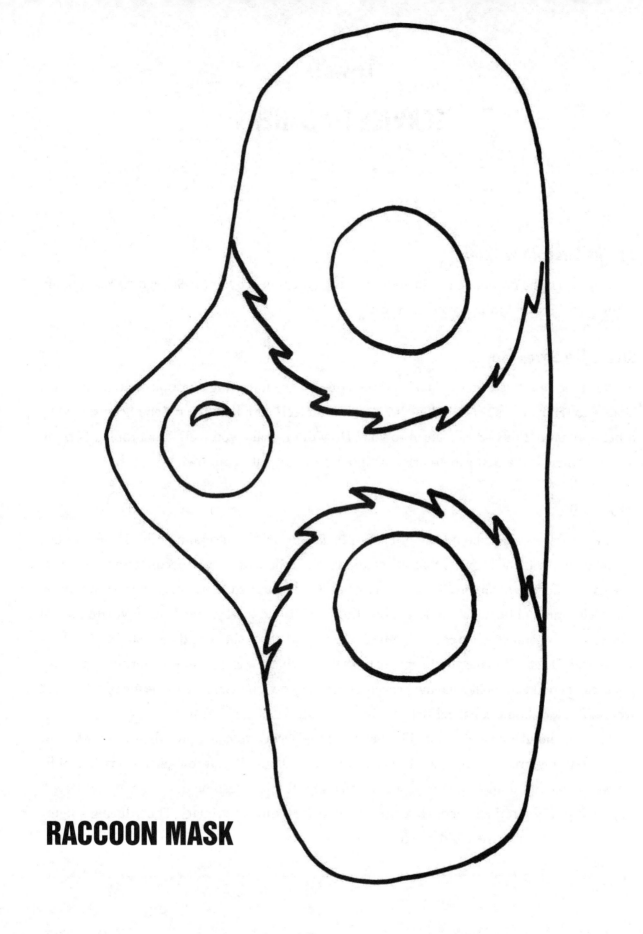

RACCOON MASK

Lesson 17

SERVICE TO OTHERS

For the Strength of Youth

Read what the prophet has said about serving others in the *For the Strength of Youth* book-let on page 38. Read John 13:35 and Mosiah 18:8–9.

Story: The Seven Star

Read the story "The Steven Star" and then discuss the following questions: Have you had a chance to serve others before? How did it make you feel? As a family, have you been served by others? What did this service mean to you? How did it make you feel? The prophet is right. Serving others is the best way to bring happiness and joy into your own life.

The Steven Star

Steven was worried about his mother. She had been sick for several months. His father had put a bed in the living room so that she could watch Father and Steven decorate the Christmas tree and participate in all the Christmas activities. Christmas had been fun even though Mother was sick. She had been so excited about the tree. It had always been her favorite part of Christmas. Sometimes when Steven sat beside her on her bed, she would say, "Steven, just look at that star. Doesn't it make you happy just to see it? When I wake up in the morning and open my eyes, there it is. It is like having heaven in our very own house. It reminds me of Jesus, and when I think of him I don't feel sick anymore."

Now the holidays were over and Father said they needed to take down the tree on Monday night. Steven worried about what Mother would do without the star to look at every morning. He worried about it all through sacrament meeting. It felt lonesome not to have Mother sit-ting next to him on the bench. He worried about it all during Primary. Then during singing time, Sister Pope had the children sing Steven's favorite song, "I Am like a Star." That was it!

That was Steven's answer. He could be Mother's star. He would do and say happy things all day. He would help in every way he could. Mother didn't need to be sad because the star on the Christmas tree was gone; Steven would be her star instead.

Steven didn't tell anyone about his plan. On Monday night he was quick to help Father get out the box for the ornaments and was careful taking the ornaments off the tree. He even got out the vacuum and cleaned up the pine needles that dropped off the tree when Father carried it out to the trash.

The next morning the house seemed empty without all the beautiful Christmas decorations. But Steven remembered his plan. He looked for ways to help and serve all day long. He brought Mother her favorite magazine to read. He got her a drink of water when it was time to take her medicine. He read her his favorite picture book. He made his bed and cleaned his room even though Mother couldn't come upstairs to see it. He sang Primary songs to Mother to help her fall asleep and he played quietly while she was resting.

All week Steven tried hard to be helpful and happy just like a star would be. Sometimes he would hum his favorite song just so he could remember. On Saturday morning, Father sat in the living room with Mother while she ate her breakfast.

Father said, "Do you miss the tree, dear? I know how much you liked looking at the star."

Mother looked at Steven and smiled. "I don't miss the star on the Christmas tree. I have my very own star that is shining brightly. My special star makes me smile and reminds me of Jesus. With all this help, I know I will be better soon."

Steven felt such a warm, good feeling inside he thought he must be glowing just like a real star. Then the Steven Star gave Mother a great big hug.

Role-Play: The Good Samaritan

Gather items such as bathrobes, towels, and scarves to make simple costumes for the role-play activity of the good Samaritan.

Act out the story of the good Samaritan. You can review the story first in Luke 10:30–37. You will need the following characters: the traveler, a thief (or thieves), a priest, a Levite, a Samaritan, and the innkeeper. (If your family is large, someone could even play the part of the donkey that the traveler rides on.)

When you have finished the role play, tell the family that the Savior told this story in answer to the question, "Who is my neighbor?" What does this story teach us about who our neighbors are? Whom should we serve? Emphasize that our neighbors can be anyone in need, people that we don't know as well as those on our street and even those in our own home.

Game: Service Scavenger Hunt

Copy the Service Scavenger Hunt lists (see page 94) and cut them apart so there are enough for each member of the family.

Hold a Service Scavenger Hunt. Give each family member the list of service activities. When Dad says "Go," the family races around individually or in teams to complete five tasks on the list. The first person or team to complete five tasks and report to Dad is the winner.

Activity: The "Star" Treatment

Make some star-shaped sugar cookies and deliver them to someone in your ward or neighborhood. You may want to pray as a family to decide who needs to receive a special treat to lift their spirits. Include a note that says, "You are stars to us!" with the cookies. Deliver the plate, ring the doorbell, and run!

Activity: Service Star

Make a Service Star by cutting a star shape out of cardboard and covering it with tinfoil.

Show the family the special Service Star. One person will start by performing some small act of service for another member of the family, such as making the bed, doing chores, leaving a loving note under a pillow, picking up shoes, etc. When the first person has finished doing an act of service for someone else, he or she leaves the star on top of that individual's bed. If you find the star on your bed, it is your turn to do some service for someone else and leave the star for that person to find. See how many good feelings you can create in the family with the Service Star throughout the next week.

Commitment

Bear your testimony of the importance of charity and service. You may want to have younger children put a sticker or draw a smiley face on page 38 in the *For the Strength of Youth* booklet. Older family members could choose to write their feelings about service or ideas about service they would like to perform in the future in the booklet or in their journals.

Treat: Star Mint Brownies

Make mint brownies using your favorite boxed brownie mix. Spread two-thirds of the brownie batter in a greased pan. Add a layer of unwrapped York Peppermint Patties laid side by side. Cover with the rest of the brownie mix and bake according to the package directions. Use a cookie cutter to cut the brownies into stars. Service brings light into people's lives just like stars do. We can shine like stars in following Jesus and serving others.

Service Scavenger Hunt List

Wash a window

Make a bed

Clean a mirror

Tidy up a room

Fold or put away some laundry

Empty or load the dishwasher

Sweep the floor in one room

Vacuum a room

Sweep the front porch

Dust one room

Service Scavenger Hunt List

Wash a window

Make a bed

Clean a mirror

Tidy up a room

Fold or put away some laundry

Empty or load the dishwasher

Sweep the floor in one room

Vacuum a room

Sweep the front porch

Dust one room

Service Scavenger Hunt List

Wash a window

Make a bed

Clean a mirror

Tidy up a room

Fold or put away some laundry

Empty or load the dishwasher

Sweep the floor in one room

Vacuum a room

Sweep the front porch

Dust one room

Service Scavenger Hunt List

Wash a window

Make a bed

Clean a mirror

Tidy up a room

Fold or put away some laundry

Empty or load the dishwasher

Sweep the floor in one room

Vacuum a room

Sweep the front porch

Dust one room

Lesson 18

GO FORWARD WITH FAITH

Story: Next Year in Zion

Tell the story "Next Year in Zion." Ask your family what caused John to keep going even though the trek over the plains was so difficult. He had faith and a conviction he would eventually reach Zion. So what is faith? Faith is our belief in God and his Son, Jesus Christ. Faith is a belief in the plan of salvation and the gospel. We have faith that our prayers are answered and that we are here on earth for a purpose. Having strong faith helps us endure hard things and helps us live the standards found in the *For the Strength of Youth* booklet. It helps us to go forward.

Next Year in Zion

This is a true story based on the life of John Rowley, great-grandfather of the author's husband.

John was freezing cold. It was hard to keep his teeth from chattering as he moved slowly back and forth in front of the camp. John was only fifteen, but all the able men and boys took turns guarding the camp at night. It didn't matter if they were cold or sick. The guarding had to be done.

John was the man of his family, so he took his responsibility more seriously than some boys his age. His pa had died back in England. John didn't think about England very much anymore. He thought about Zion instead. He had first heard the word from Wilford Woodruff, the Mormon missionary who had come to teach the United Brethren. Zion sounded like heaven. A place where everyone shared equally and where there were no rich or poor. A place where each man could achieve his dreams and where working hard would bring success. John wanted to leave for Zion that same night.

He had been eleven years old then and working in a factory for a cruel boss who would cuff his ears until they bled if he did something wrong. Mama cried when she saw the blood on his ears, but there wasn't anything she could do. The money had to be earned somehow.

It took three years after the family had been baptized before they could leave for America. Three long years of working and saving and praying and even then they still needed money from the Perpetual Emigration Fund. John thanked God every day for the Saints in Utah who had helped his family to come to Zion.

It was the Book of Mormon that helped John get through his father's death and the wait to come to Zion. Mama loved to read the Book of Mormon. John could remember watching the candles burn down as they talked into the night about the prophet and how they wanted to see him. John had known that the Book of Mormon was true when his mama first read its pages aloud. Even on the trail, pushing a handcart day after day, he could still remember the warmth of those nights. His thoughts of Zion and the Book of Mormon were like a fire to him. They kept him warm inside even when he was cold outside and didn't think he could move another step.

The thought of the cold brought John back to the night around him. The snow crunched under his feet. He could hear the moans of the sick and the dying as they lay under the handcarts in the crusty snow. Every night more people died. John knew that they were in a better place and that God had a purpose for everything. Still, he didn't want to die before they reached Zion. The food rations were very small now. There was no telling how long it would take the Saints to reach the Salt Lake Valley. They were traveling so slowly, their energy spent, with barely enough strong men to dig the shallow graves that littered the sides of the trail behind them.

If only he could just lie down for a moment, just long enough to get warm, and then he could finish his guard duty. Just to lie down for a minute until his teeth stopped chattering and his head stopped pounding. Just a few minutes of sleep and then he would be ready to march on to Zion.

John lay down in the snow and soon fell asleep. When the guard came to replace him, the man thought John was dead. He kicked the body and John moaned. His hair had frozen to the ground and they had to cut him free before they could carry him to a sick wagon.

Miraculously, John recovered and he was there to greet the rescuers who arrived to help the Willie Handcart Company. He was even well enough to help carry women and children across the Sweetwater River as they finished their journey to Salt Lake. The river was so cold that his mother had to cut his clothes off him at the end of the day, but John made it to Zion.

Even with all his trials, John never lost faith in Zion. He arrived in the Salt Lake Valley on November 9, 1856. For the rest of his life, John Rowley was faithful to The Church of Jesus Christ of Latter-day Saints and made every sacrifice asked of him by the prophet Brigham Young to build Zion and strengthen the kingdom of God on the earth.

For the Strength of Youth

Read what the prophet has said about going forward with faith in the *For the Strength of Youth* booklet on page 40. Each paragraph on that page includes one challenge of something we should each do. See if you can identify and highlight each challenge. For example, in the first paragraph, we are asked to review the pamphlet often, with this question in mind: "Am I living the way the Lord wants me to live?" Once you have identified each challenge, read page 41. These are the promises that the Lord gives us for living these standards. See if each family member can list at least one promised blessing for living the standards. Then read 2 Nephi 31:16–21 about pressing forward on the straight and narrow path.

Game: Go Forward with FAITH

Prepare ahead by copying the letters to spell out F-A-I-T-H (see pagse 99–103). Each family member will need all five letters.

Play the "Go Forward with FAITH" game. Give each player a set of cards that spell out F-A-I-T-H. Have everyone stand on one side of the living room. Players take turns answering the question for the letter F. When they have answered, they can toss their letter F in front of them and then jump to it. Throw as far as you think you can jump but no farther. If you jump short of the card, you must return to your previous spot and answer the question again. When each person has moved to his or her new position, continue with the A card and so on. Play until each person has landed on their H card.

Game Questions

F: Tell your **Feelings** about your **Family** and Jesus Christ.

A: Tell what **Actions** you can do to strenthen your faith.

I: Faith is needed **In** obeying which commandments?

T: Share your **Testimony** about the Book of Mormon and the prophet.

H: Tell how faith **Helps** you in your life.

Commitment

Bear your testimony of the power that faith has had in your life. You may want to have younger children put a sticker or draw a smiley face on page 41 of the *For the Strength of Youth* booklet. Older family members could choose to write their feelings about faith and their commitment to show increased faith in certain areas in the booklet or in their journals.

Treat: Covered Wagon Cookies

Make covered wagons by using a dab of frosting to stick a marshmallow onto a bite-sized Snickers bar. Use another dab of frosting to attach chocolate-cookie wheels and a pretzel-stick wagon tongue. Use animal crackers as oxen to complete your wagon. Remember the faith of the pioneers that helped them cross the plains. Like them, we can also have great faith.

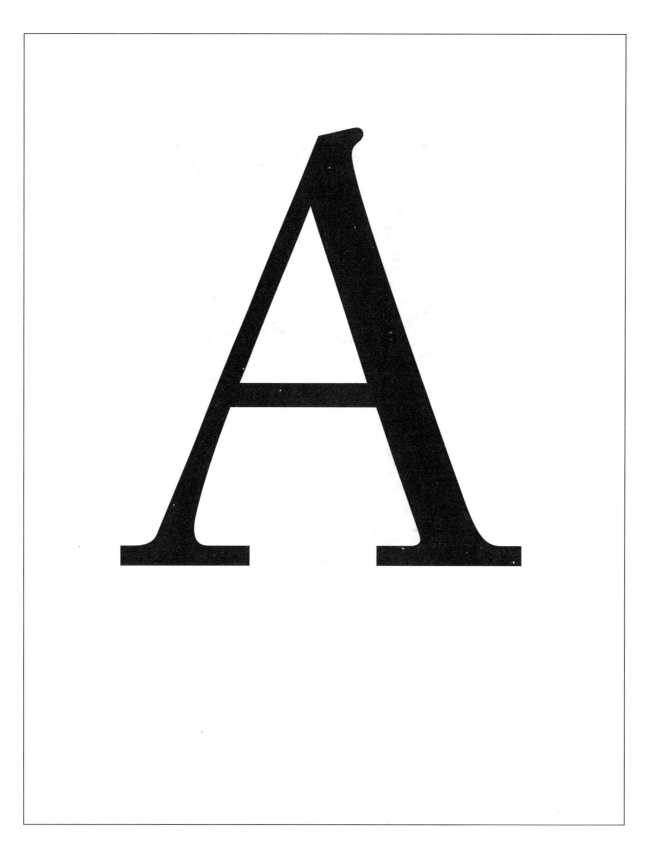

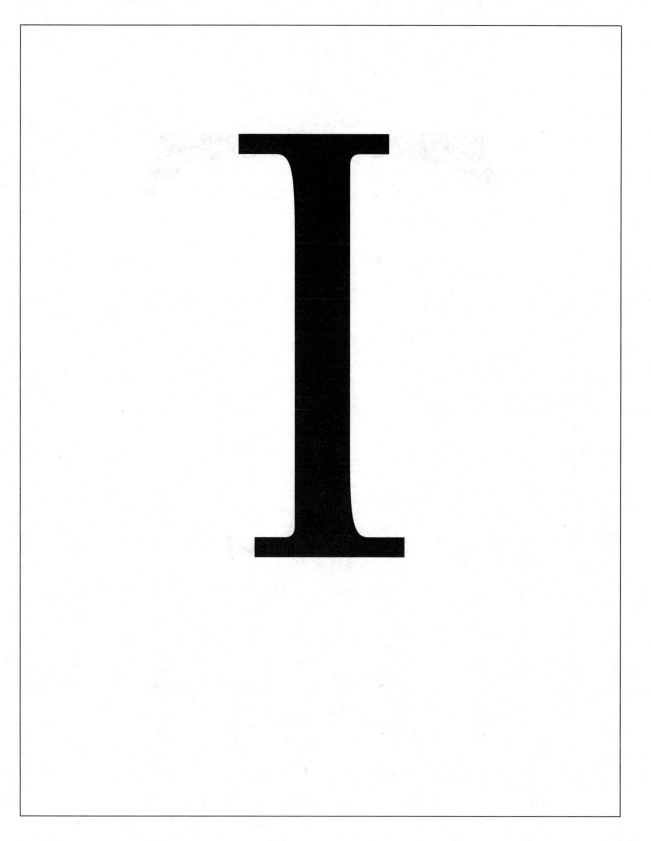

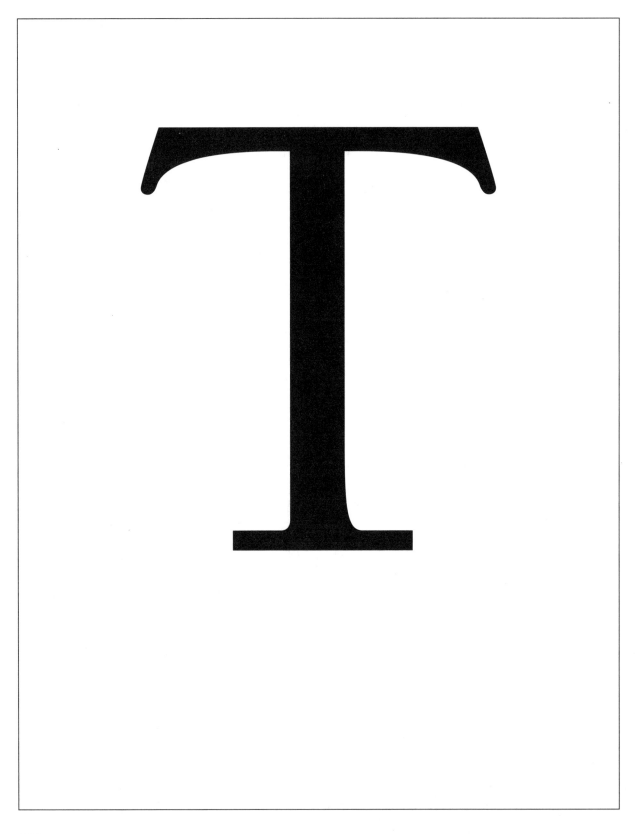

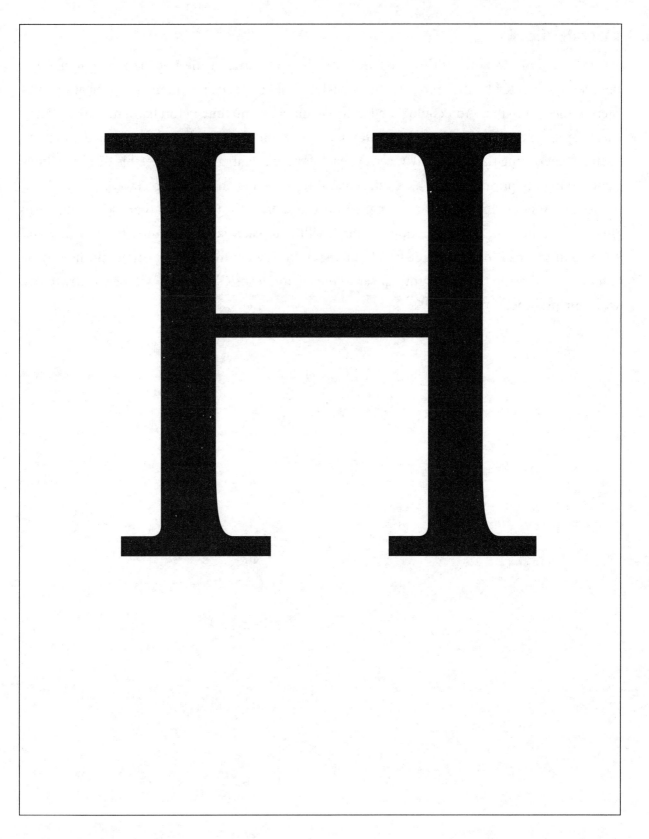

Congratulations!

You have now shared with your family all the standards in the *For the Strength of Youth* booklet. As directed by the Spirit, you may wish to hold a special testimony meeting after completing these activities. You could give family members some time beforehand to look through their copies of the *For the Strength of Youth* booklet to find the principle that means the most to them. Then during the testimony meeting, each family member could share his or her feelings about living the principle they have chosen and the blessings they have received.

At the end of the testimony meeting, you could share your testimony that the principles in this booklet are true and that following them will help each family member to be happy and successful in this life. Encourage family members to review the booklet often and live by its teachings. If they do they will grow closer to the Savior, Jesus Christ, and will be worthy to live with him and their family forever.